When Teachers

Face Themselves

A PUBLICATION OF THE

HORACE MANN-LINCOLN INSTITUTE OF SCHOOL EXPERIMENTATION

TEACHERS COLLEGE, COLUMBIA UNIVERSITY

When Teachers
Face Themselves

ARTHUR T. JERSILD

Professor of Education, Teachers College

Columbia University

TEACHERS COLLEGE PRESS

TEACHERS COLLEGE, COLUMBIA UNIVERSITY

The work underlying this book was done under the auspices of the Horace Mann-Lincoln Institute of School Experimentation in association with Dr. Jane Beasley and with the assistance of Miss Leah Ann Green, Dr. Jeanne Noble, and Dr. Ann Walsh.

Foreword

This book is Professor Jersild's most recent study of the relation between self-understanding and education. His discussion centers on the teacher whose "understanding and acceptance of himself is the most important requirement in any effort he makes to help students to know themselves and to gain healthy attitudes of self-acceptance." Professor Jersild sees no short cut to self-understanding, but his interviews and conversations with hundreds of teachers suggest to him the seriousness of their search for intimate and personal meaning in what they are doing. All too often, this quest is pursued under a heavy burden of anxiety and loneliness and hostility. Professor Jersild describes what this means. He stresses the hopefulness, however, and not the discouragement in what teachers are doing to face and understand themselves. His argument is, in most instances, inferred from the kind of data a psychologist naturally seeks. These data are reproduced in considerable detail in the Appendix. In the text itself, however, the author does not hesitate to speculate with great sensitivity upon the more subtle meanings of the data.

Professor Jersild writes with disarming lucidity about many abstruse conceptions. He has the courage to discuss forthrightly important topics that are generally skirted in discussions about education. I believe that *When Teachers Face Themselves* will help any but the most recalcitrant reader to face himself more realistically.

STEPHEN M. COREY, *Director*
Horace Mann-Lincoln Institute
of School Experimentation

Contents

CONTENTS

When Teachers

Face Themselves

ONE

Introduction

This book is concerned with the strivings, satisfactions, hopes, and heartaches that pervade the teacher's life and work. It deals with aspirations and struggles which large numbers of teachers have described and which all of us share. It searches into meanings we all seek to embrace. While it centers on teachers, most of what it contains applies to people in other walks of life. It has been written for teachers with the help of teachers. The research findings underlying it are noted mainly in the Appendix. The emphasis in the text is on what these findings mean from a personal point of view.

This is a personal document, for the voices of those who helped prepare it speak through it. Many of them, in the course of the study, glowed with the dedication of their calling, bristled with anger, trembled with fear, wept as only troubled souls can weep. Many of them unveiled a little of the pride and shame and tenderness people usually keep concealed from one another, and they also voiced hopeful expectations of things to be. They spoke in the language through which people reveal their weaknesses. This is also the language of humility and courage and kindness, through which people reveal their strength.

The author and his associates have also tried to speak with this voice, for the concerns expressed by the people in this study are our concerns. Many of them said they have been anxious—so have we. Many spoke of their loneliness—we, too, have tasted the loneliness that flows through so many of the tides of life. Many said they search for meaning—we, too, are involved in this search. Many expressed faith and hope; unless we shared this hope, there would be no point in undertaking a study such as this, and it would be foolish to remain in the teaching profession.

Background and Theme

This book is one of a series of writings carrying the theme that education should help children and adults to know themselves and to develop healthy attitudes of self-acceptance. The present volume considers what the concepts of self-understanding and self-acceptance mean for teachers. It discusses concerns teachers feel they must face in their personal and professional lives when they examine the meaning of what they are and what they teach and when they seek to share the personal problems of their pupils.

This is the fourth installment in a continuing inquiry. The inquiry began with a theoretical statement concerning the meaning of the concept of selfhood for education (24).[1] The next phase of the inquiry was centered on children—what

[1] Numbers in parentheses refer to items in the Bibliography, pages 139–141.

they think and feel about themselves and what problems teachers encounter when they try to help children to face themselves (23). The inquiry into the role of the teacher was continued in a third undertaking, consisting of a workshop for high school teachers of psychology (27). Other writings by the author dealing with theoretical and practical considerations related to the theme of this book are listed in the Bibliography.

All of the work that has preceded this book—in classrooms with children, in conferences with teachers, in the literature dealing with the theoretical issues involved—has emphasized one fact. The teacher's understanding and acceptance of himself is the most important requirement in any effort he makes to help students to know themselves and to gain healthy attitudes of self-acceptance. The crucial question that has emerged again and again is this: *What does this effort to help students mean in a distinctly intimate, personal way in the teacher's own life?* This book endeavors to explore some of the issues that must be explored when we seek an answer to this question.

It has become increasingly clear over the years, as the work in this inquiry proceeded, that self-understanding requires something quite different from the methods, study plans, and skills of a "know-how" sort that are usually emphasized in education. Methods and techniques, group work, role playing, and other devices are useful at certain points. But these educational techniques are not what is primarily needed. They can be used merely as a kind of external manipulation. When so used, they do not further and may even defeat the purpose we are seeking here. What is needed is a more personal kind of searching, which will enable the teacher to identify his own concerns and to share the concerns of his students.

Major Concerns

In this book we have drawn heavily on an empirical study (described on pages 13–19) of the personal concerns of teachers. Among the concerns voiced by those who participated in the study, two especially stand out. One of these is the problem of meaning. Many teachers have felt a need to examine the significance of the life they are living and the meaning of the work they are doing in the name of scholarship and education. These people do not deny that learning is good. They would all agree that it is a fine thing to encourage scholarly pursuits, to do research, to acquaint the young with our cultural heritage. They accept the idea that education should help people to use the methods of science and to think logically about current problems. But they recognize that these undertakings are often rather empty. There is much that is meaningless along the academic road, from the kindergarten to the doctor's degree. Much of what goes on consists of scholarly motions, lacking the vital spark of personal concern.

The search for meaning is not a search for an abstract body of knowledge, or even for a concrete body of knowledge. It is a distinctly personal search. The one who makes it raises intimate personal questions: What really counts, for me? What values am I seeking? What, in my existence as a person, in my relations with others, in my work as a teacher, is of real concern to me, perhaps of ultimate concern to me? In my teaching I seek to transmit the meanings others have found in their search for truth, and that is good as far as it goes. But as I try to help young people to discover meaning, have I perhaps evaded the question of what life might mean to me? How can I, in my study and my teaching and in the countless topics that engage my thought, find a home within myself?

This search for meaning is, of course, an ancient search. It is true that the lessons we are taught in school and college usually center on objective facts rather than personal meanings. They tell us how man, through the ages, has penetrated into the nature of things as he looks upward and outward upon the world in which he lives. But now and then, also, there are teachers who tell us to look inward. Through the ages, voices have again and again been raised, calling man home to himself, calling upon him once more to face the timeless question: Who and what and why am I?

When the teachers in this study raised the question of meaning, they raised a question as old as the human race. It is therefore ironic when people say, as many have said concerning the theme of this book and of the works that preceded it, that here is something "new," that the "latest" idea in education is that the learner should seek to know himself. This idea is not new at all. Man's inquiry into the meaning of his existence goes back to the time when he first began to think, to wonder, and to dream. In each human life this same search is taken up anew when a child, in his first groping endeavors, seeks to discover the how and the why. Each child joins in this timeless search when he first begins to ask: What does it matter? What difference does it make? Such questions are old, but they are not always welcome. Many children learn to stop putting them to others, and there are many, as they move on in school, who think they have learned even to stop asking themselves. But questions such as these are bound to arise again and again as long as there is life.

The question of meaning arises when a teacher looks inward upon himself and also when he looks outward upon the world about him. He sees how boldly scientists proceed to explore the properties of the physical world and yet how baffled the great ones among them are by questions concerning man's inner life. He sees that we now have machines in which a man can move at supersonic speed—and then realizes that such speed does not make it easier for him to find himself, or to lose himself. He sees the fabulous strength man has gained by breaking the secret of atomic power—and then he asks: Does he also have the strength to face himself? He sees that medical science has increased the average life span by many years—but he asks: Does life acquire meaning, or acquire richer meaning, because death has been somewhat delayed?

A teacher's questions about meaning do not become less insistent when he turns from the world of science to the world of religion, for even here questions of meaning arise. According to one recent investigation, about nine out of ten people in the population that was studied professed religious beliefs, but only about one in six held to these beliefs in a way that seemed to make a vital difference within the privacy of his own life (46). We can ask: Were the tests adequate? Are these proportions typical? What findings analogous to these might emerge if we could make a similar study of scholars and educators, asking: What do these people formally profess, and what does it actually mean to them? How much of what they say and know is lip service? How much is scholarly posture, after the manner of an actor who strikes the correct pose and recites the proper lines? How much is interwoven with their total way of life? We do not know what the answer would be. Actually, it does not matter much what the answer might be as it pertains to *others*. The thing that matters to the individual scholar and teacher is what these questions mean for himself. It is from this distinctly personal point of view that many of the teachers in the present study raised questions concerning the meaning of their own lives and works.

The search for meaning is, as has been said, a distinctly personal search. It is not just a scholarly enterprise, although the pursuit of learning is an important aspect of it. It can be shared, to some extent, with others, and people can draw encouragement from the fact that others, like them, feel uneasy about the emptiness of much of what is done in the name of learning. But the real encounter with the problem must take place in the privacy of each person's own life. Even then, as D. H. Lawrence (37) has pointed out, the meaning a person can embrace within his known self may be only a little clearing in the forest. But a little clearing is infinitely greater than no clearing at all, and it is better (according to the philosophy underlying this book) to dwell in such a clearing, and to work in it, with things that count, than just to go through the motions. It is better to have such a home in the wilderness than to move through life in a mechanical way, unreached, untouched, and unmoved by what one learns and uninvolved in what one teaches.

The second pervasive concern with which this book deals is anxiety. Chapter Two discusses the way anxiety permeates the lives of teachers and their pupils. *It takes the position that the concept of anxiety should be regarded as an essential topic in all teacher-training programs.*

One of the most impressive features of this study was the response teachers made when the subject of anxiety was discussed. Many at once related it to their personal experience and were eager to explore its meaning in their own lives. Others, of course, did not see the subject as having any relevance for them.

The writer had not expected so much readiness to face the

problem of anxiety. While there is anxiety in the lives of all of us, we also build defenses against it, and one common defense is to see anxiety as something that affects others, not ourselves. A similar defense is to see it as an interesting psychological problem, not as a pervasive reality in our own lives. There are many who seem to succeed quite well, for rather long periods of time, in avoiding direct awareness of their anxiety. There are others who do not recognize anxiety except dimly, at times, through feeling vaguely depressed, edgy, driven, irritable, or uneasy, or through having a tendency to become angry about little things, or to feel abused or rejected when mildly criticized, or to hurt others, or to feel impatient, or restless, or defensive, or through a need always to be right, or to say something, or to impress everyone, or to be endlessly busy and on the go.

The people who have the courage to face anxiety and who seek to explore its meaning accept the fact that they, like all people, are to some degree anxious. They recognize that many teachers and students have lived with the burden of anxiety day after day, scarcely knowing that the burden might be lightened. They realize that schools and colleges have usually offered them little in the way of help except academic activities that sidestep anxiety, or perhaps even increase it.

When a person pursues the subject of anxiety, he may find that he is among those who have been involved in a long struggle against awareness of being anxious. Those who make this struggle may to all appearances be well-organized, busy persons, involved in a round of meetings, conferences, homework, community projects, research, and professional activity. On the surface, such people may appear to be leading rich and productive lives. They may say that they like their teaching, that they find educational pursuits rewarding. But if the inner

8

dimensions of their personalities could be examined, many would show a large amount of tension, appearing, say, in disproportionate resentment, competitiveness, discouragement, efforts to impress or to placate, to play the game and to play it safe. Many of them, in their anxiety, probably place excessive demands on themselves and others, have inordinate needs for approval, persistently avoid writings or discussions dealing with subjects that carry unpleasant reminders of something they do not wish to face, or now and then are swept by intense waves of anger against themselves, or by unaccountable longings or feelings of depression.

There are, on the other hand, people who have faced—or, as many persons in this study indicated, wish to face—the realization that one cannot live without becoming anxious. They may know that they share the experience of anxiety with all mankind and realize that, by accepting it in themselves and others, by living with it and seeking to understand its texture, they may be able to live with less strain and learn to be more compassionate in their view of themselves and more humane in their relations with others.

There are other pressing personal concerns that teachers reveal when they push aside the curtain behind which people in the teaching profession, as in other professions, commonly conceal their inner selves. Many teachers expressed a deep loneliness, a loneliness related to the fact that so often (among teachers as among others) there is little mutual understanding or community of feeling with associates or even with "friends." Many were disturbed by their hostile tendencies— tendencies that prevail in the life of everyone. There are few unforbidden, frank and direct channels for expressing hostility in education, but much of what is done in the name of education or scholarship is, indirectly, a means of venting hostility.

We fall in with institutionalized expressions of hostility when, for example, we unhesitatingly inflict hurt on others, get children by the millions into situations where they will fail—and we know in advance they will fail, know that the circumstances are such that they cannot help but fail and get no benefit from the pain of failing again and again. We vent hostility in education when we snobbishly scorn those who are less intelligent or less learned than ourselves, or when we join in the antagonism that often prevails between colleges of liberal arts and schools of education. Such institutionalized manifestations of hostility were not, however, the central concern expressed by the people who took part in this study. The problem of hostility was, to those who identified it, a distinctly personal problem, and they wished to face it as such.

Closely related to the problem of coming to terms with hostility is an even larger concern, which many teachers expressed—a concern about emotion in general. Many expressed a desire for insight that might enable them to draw more freely upon their feelings, or might enable them to know what their real feelings were. Freedom to think is a perennial issue in academic life, but an even more significant issue in the lives of many is freedom to feel: freedom to allow feeling to surge within themselves without being compelled to snuff it out and deny it; freedom to experience the full impact of fear (and who is not afraid?); of hate (who is not swayed by it?); of tenderness (who does not possess it?); of joy (what person does not have some capacity for it?); of compassion (who does not own a rich potential store?).

Other concerns expressed include the burden of conformity, under which many labor (in the name of being sensible and socially well adjusted); the oppressive load imposed by striving to live up to an impossible ideal—a kind of striving some educators cultivate as though it were a virtue; the difficulty many have in "being themselves" when dealing with someone who wields authority or who is, to them, a symbol of authority; the concerns many have in the sphere of sex.

In an earlier book the writer, in commenting on the poignant and eager way children reveal their problems to teachers they trust, said that one can hear through them a cry of pain, a plea for help arising from millions of troubled people. Perhaps this statement seems extreme, but it was true in its context. The same statement can as truly be made in the present context. When one works individually with teachers and gives them a chance to share a little of that secret burden each of us usually bears alone, one can hear this same cry of pain and plea for help. This does not mean that pain is the only or the predominant condition in their lives. They know joy as well as pain. But it does mean that many who usually find it necessary to conceal their troubles and their hurts would like to find an opportunity to share them.

The hopeful thing about it is that they have the courage to utter this cry and to phrase this plea. Indeed, students in education courses are prepared, under appropriate circumstances, to reveal needs in their personal and professional lives that schools of education have barely begun to meet. Students dare to ask for more than colleges following the usual safe and impersonal channels of education have dared to give.

Underlying Sources

THEORETICAL ROOTS

While this book centers on personal concerns, it is rooted in several theoretical areas. One of these is developmental psychology, particularly as it pertains to growth and to the conditions influencing the emotional lives of children and adults. As one studies developmental psychology, through writings or through observation of people, one is reminded often and eloquently of the power of the human being's impulse to grow. This impulse is strongest in the young, but it is strong also in older people, for as long as there is life there is a chance for growth in the inner dimensions of personality. Developmental psychology reveals how boldly children venture into the business of life, how often they are frightened, hurt, and bruised, how strong the surge of life is. From developmental psychology we learn how great is the human capacity for self-repair. This capacity persists even though a person has been deeply wounded at one stage or another in his life.

A second influence on this book comes from psychoanalytic psychology, especially from the works of Horney (15–19), Sullivan (48–50), and Fromm (9, 10) and the light these have shed on issues raised in an earlier day by Freud (6–8), Adler (1), and Jung (29–31). These writers have greatly increased our understanding of the difficulties that beset a person in his search for himself. They also draw attention to resources for growth and to sources of hope on which man can rely.

There are important areas of human experience that an analyst or a therapist can work on but a teacher cannot. The genius who can show how the full range of the benefits of psychoanalysis and psychotherapy might be incorporated into the regular educational process has not come along. However, many of the common areas are already obvious. There is much in the professional work of a good therapist that can also be made part of the work of the teacher.

A third influence that runs through this book comes from philosophical inquiries into the meaning of man's existence, especially those of Kierkegaard (32–36) and Tillich (52, 53).

Kierkegaard's explorations of the concept of selfhood, the nature of the human struggle, the conditions of man's anxiety, the personal character of meaning, and the subjective dimensions of truth have anticipated much that is now in the forefront of contemporary thought. The issues with which he dealt have been echoed again and again by the students, teachers, and colleagues who took part in this study. Tillich, likewise, voices many of their concerns when he speaks of man's predicament in facing the problems of emptiness and rejection and inquires into the nature of man's courage to be himself.

THE EMPIRICAL STUDY

Several thousands of people helped in one way or another in the undertaking this book discusses. The help came through written statements, opinion polls, lengthy personal conferences, and the sharing of clinical experiences. Some of the participants were colleagues and students who have undergone the experience of psychotherapy and who have been seeking to discover what this might mean in their work as teachers. Most of those who took part were students (in large part, teachers engaged in part-time or full-time graduate work) in courses taught by the writer. In these courses a position familiar to those who have read earlier writings in this series was discussed. It is reviewed briefly here:

An essential function of good education is to help the growing child to know himself and to grow in healthy attitudes of self-acceptance.

A teacher cannot make much headway in understanding others or in helping others to understand themselves unless he is endeavoring to understand himself. If he is not engaged in this endeavor, he will continue to see those whom he teaches through the bias and distortions of his own unrecognized needs, fears, desires, anxieties, hostile impulses, and so on.

The process of gaining knowledge of self and the struggle for self-fulfillment and self-acceptance is not something an instructor *teaches* others. It is not something he does *to* or *for* them. It is something in which he himself must be involved.

The study involved four procedures: a survey of reactions to the idea of self-understanding as a basic aim in education; a series of personal conferences; a survey of personal problems as revealed by written responses to an inventory; and ratings and evaluations of lectures and discussions dealing with various aspects of self-understanding. The book draws heavily on the findings that emerged from these procedures; it is not, however, bound by them.

Response to the Idea of Self-Understanding.—In the first survey, over a thousand teachers and students of education were asked to express their views anonymously concerning the concept of self-understanding in education and its implications for them. They were also asked to indicate what they felt was needed most if education for self-understanding was to become part of the education of every child. They had a choice, for example, of asking for workshops, of indicating that more attention should be given to distinctly personal and emotional aspects of the teacher's work, or of expressing a desire for personal help through means such as group therapy. (The questions used in this part of the study and a tabulation of responses appear in Appendix A.)

Eleven groups, numbering from 33 to 149 and totaling 1,032 persons, responded to these questions. The groups included classes taught by the writer, a few classes taught by other instructors, and the faculty of a high school. In all these groups, the concepts of self-understanding and self-

14

acceptance had been discussed, but the emphasis varied considerably according to the views of the instructor. The time given to the theme ranged from a short twenty-minute talk in one group to many class sessions in some of the others.

The responses of these people indicate that *the idea that the school should promote self-understanding is, in theory at least, a very acceptable one.* In most groups over ninety per cent indicated that they thought it was "promising and worth trying."

Likewise, nine out of ten people indicated that the idea that understanding of others is tied to self-understanding was, to them, a "promising" and not an unpleasant or distasteful concept.

Fewer people, but still from one half to two thirds, indicated that the idea of self-understanding was or might be "most significant" in their own professional education.

The most significant feature of this set of questions consisted of four options relating to the kind of personal help the people desired or the kind of personal commitment they would make in an effort to put this idea to work. One option was workshops, special courses, etc. (which might mean very much or very little involvement). Another option was provision for discussing personal and emotional issues (implying a personal commitment but permitting the participant to keep himself at arm's length in the discussion). A third option was psychological services for others. This option, if chosen alone, suggests that the person sees self-understanding primarily as something other people should be helped to achieve. The fourth option was personal help such as might be gotten from group therapy. Of all the options, this indicates the strongest commitment and the deepest involvement. It was permissible to check one or more than one of the four options.

15

When a count was made of those who chose either the option of therapy or the discussion of personal and emotional issues, or both, the tallies showed that from about half to over four fifths of the people in the several groups had selected one or both of these options. In six of the eleven groups, over seventy per cent made such a choice. Between about one fifth and one half in each group indicated a desire for help such as might be gotten from group therapy.

What do these figures mean?

They mean that at least as far as verbal assent is concerned, people in groups such as those canvassed here lean strongly toward incorporating the concept of self-understanding into the educational program. The climate of opinion is also favorable to the idea that this will require teachers to face personal issues in their own lives—through therapy or discussion of "personal and emotional issues"—in a manner that differs from the usual academic work.

The figures do not reveal how many people really would take the initiative in becoming deeply involved in a discussion of their personal and emotional concerns if the necessary provisions for doing so were made. Neither do we know how many would take the plunge into therapy if the opportunity were actually offered. The writer's general observation has been that when some kind of group work with a personal reference, explicitly planned to foster self-understanding, is offered in connnection with courses attended by the student body represented in this study, there are many volunteers. Due to a variety of factors, such as reluctance when actually faced with an opportunity and difficulties in timing, scheduling, and staffing, the number is usually smaller than that of the people who, in this survey, indicated a desire for such work. Moreover, this kind of group activity, while it seems to be significant, also falls short of a systematic group therapy under the guidance of a professionally trained therapist or analyst.

We cannot assume that other groups in a teacher-training institution would respond as these groups have responded. Groups of undergraduates probably would react differently. People who have had no contact with the concept underlying this book and no interest even in taking courses or in coming to talks that might deal with this concept would probably respond differently.

It does seem to be significant, however, that a favorable response was shown, for example, by a group of high school teachers (Group B) who had had only brief contact with the writer's point of view, at a meeting held at the school at the end of a busy day, and by a group of curriculum majors (Group G), who had no special reason for favoring a distinctly psychological approach.

Personal Conferences.—It was suggested that those who had indicated, in the first part of the study, that they would like to have some personal help might come once or oftener for personal conferences of an hour or more to tell what they had in mind. Eighty people came to be interviewed, some of them several times. In the interviews, which were conducted by people who had had considerable experience in counseling individuals and who had been involved to some extent in the practical aspects of therapeutic work, most of them revealed themselves quite openly and freely. In addition, during the five years this study has been in progress, several hundred other people, students in courses taught by the writer, have disclosed some of their problems and reactions in written individual and group reports.

The Personal Issues Inventory.—We were now ready for

the third part of the study. The records of interviews were examined for recurring personal problems and concerns, and the language those interviewed had used in expressing their problems was extracted from them. The problems and concerns revealed fell into a number of categories, about thirty in all, but it was decided to focus attention on the nine that appeared to receive the greatest emphasis: meaninglessness, loneliness, sex, attitudes toward authority, freedom to feel, feelings of homelessness, feelings of hopelessness, hostility, distress because of discrepancy between the "real" self and the demands and expectations imposed by self or others.

On the basis of the interviews, an instrument (shown in Appendix B) was devised which included thirty-six statements of problems or symptoms, four in each of the nine categories listed above. This instrument is referred to hereafter as the Personal Issues Inventory. On the left side of each page, statements of personal problems were given as examples of "What others have said." On the right side of each page there was provision for responding under the heading, "My own feeling, as I consider what I'd like to understand about myself, is that . . ." Several choices were offered under this heading. The respondent could check "I've felt this way, and it's one of the areas in which I probably need help in understanding myself"; or, "I've felt this way, but I don't particularly see it as an issue on which I need help"; or, "This has not been an issue in my life"; or, "I'm not sure."

This instrument was administered to two groups of students (a total of 229 people) near the end of the semester, after the students had had considerable opportunity to become acquainted with the theme underlying this book and to develop their attitudes toward it through class discussion, group discussions, individual conferences, and the like. Most of these people were graduate students at Teachers College, Columbia University, working for a master's or a doctor's degree. The median age was over thirty years. They represented people who specialized in a wide range of educational areas, including curriculum and teaching, guidance, nursing education, psychology, religious education, physical education, art, the teaching of social studies, language arts, and others. The larger of the two groups met on Saturday and included many part-time students who were carrying other responsibilities.

The people who responded to the Personal Issues Inventory cannot be called a random group. Originally they were a relatively unselected group within the student body as a whole, who either elected or were required to take a course in developmental psychology. They were not, in the main, people who from the start were seeking to ally themselves with the writer's views concerning the importance of the concepts of self-understanding and self-acceptance. (One of the courses had not originally carried the writer's name; the listing in the catalog had merely stated, "Instructor to Be Announced.") However, by the time the semester was nearly over, these people had had an opportunity, over a period of many weeks, to become familiar with the underlying idea and to accept or reject it.

Ratings and Evaluations.—There is an additional large body of material that has influenced the content of this book, including ratings and evaluations growing out of work with many small groups and with several large classes, reactions to specific topics introduced in classes (including the topic of anxiety), lengthy personal documents, and the like.

TWO

Anxiety

Ours is called an age of anxiety, and so it is.[1] Each age is an age of anxiety. Ever since man has been affected by the stress of conflicting tendencies within himself, he has been anxious. He is not only apprehensive about dangers and threats that overhang his physical existence; as a human being, he also bears this additional burden: he is anxious.

Man is capable of a kind of uneasiness, apprehension, depression, disturbance, or distress arising from conditions that threaten his existence from within. These feelings are usually tied to unresolved problems of the past. A person resides on

[1] This chapter, unlike most of the others, does not take its departure from empirical findings but introduces, instead, considerations pertaining to the concept of anxiety which, in the writer's judgment, need to be brought into the mainstream of educational thought. At the end of the chapter some findings pertaining to the way teachers react to this concept and its implications are commented on. A brief summary of the main quantitative findings is given in Appendix E.

I am indebted to Professors Millie Almy and Stephen M. Corey, Dr. Jane Beasley, and Professor Anne McKillop for counsel and encouragement in connection with the preparation of this chapter and those that follow.

20

an island between what has been and what is yet to be. He can glory in his past—or rue it. He can dream of his future—or dread it. The past lives in the present within most people's lives, often in the form of unresolved problems. These problems produce anxiety, especially when a person does not recognize them for what they are.

One danger man shares with other creatures is linked to a certainty that faces him from the time he is born: he will die. Life and death are close companions. Wherever life leads, death comes close behind. This closeness of life and death is terrifying to some people, and it brings moments of terror to all, young and old, at times of accident, catastrophe, or other great danger. But it is not a chief source of our anxiety. We learn to live with the prospect of dying, for usually the prospect is quite remote. He who moves most fully into life feels most removed from death. He who is least afraid of living is least afraid of dying. And he who has had a reasonably full existence would not, at any stage along life's way, go back and relive his past, even though he might wish the earlier stages had been different and even though he realizes that each new stage brings him nearer his end.

More conducive to anxiety than the certainty of physical extinction are the conflicting tendencies within man's inner life. These psychological forces that contend with one another may appear in his conscious awareness, or they may reside mainly in what some have called the unconscious, hidden, or unrecognized reaches of his life.

At the level of awareness, for example, one may recognize that to live means to venture; but a venture may go wrong and may leave regret, guilt, or some other tendency to punish oneself. Yet if one does not venture the impulse to venture still persists, so that some people are as disturbed by conflicts concerning what they have *not* done as others are by conflicts concerning what they *have* done. An example of this appeared in the present study: some people said they felt guilty about sex experiences they had had, while others said they felt guilty about sex experiences they had not had. To live means to strike some sort of balance between venturing and playing it safe—and to find a perfect balance at all times is impossible.

On the level of awareness there are also other issues that produce conflict. To live means to struggle. There is a struggle between dependency on other people and the need to be independent; the need to be accepted and approved by others and the need to assert oneself and to live a life of one's own, even if it hurts others or brings disapproval from those whose good will is very important. To live means to face the inevitable and often conflicting promptings of love and hate, producing tensions so strong at times that some people will not take the risk of loving and dare not boldly risk feeling anger, and so live uneasily in a state of outward calm built upon inner tensions. To live means also to seek acceptance and to face the possibility of rejection; to love and to take the chance of losing what one loves. These and many other alternatives are tied to living, and conflicts are bound to arise. These conflicts may lead to anxiety, which is part of the price human beings must pay for being alive.

Some theories of anxiety, which will be noted later, emphasize the role of a person's relations with others—notably with his parents when he was a child—and consequent attitudes he has concerning himself. But anxiety is linked to a larger set of circumstances than those involved in the relations between a child and his elders. Even if these relations are as good as human relations can be, it is likely that a person sooner or later (if he uses his capacities for thinking and doing) will be subject to anxiety because of the complexities and the hazards involved in his relation to himself and to the universe. The theory here is that a human being, by virtue of the nature of his faculties and limitations, will face possibilities and predicaments that will lead to anxiety.

Man is finite, yet he has a vast amount of freedom. He faces innumerable alternatives; he makes choices that, in retrospect, are right or wrong, wise or foolish. In a decision he made in the past he took one road, but, as he later sees it, he might have taken another. In his plans for the future he elects one course, but, as he sees it, he might still elect another. The more actively he avails himself of the right to choose, the more responsibility he will feel for the course he chooses. He will make choices that have consequences he cannot foresee. And the greater the realm of choice, the greater the possibility of conflict between contending desires and impulses within himself.

Man's powers are limited, but the possibilities for aspiration and action within the limits are almost staggering. He is ignorant, in a relative sense, yet his capacities for discovery are tremendous. He has every reason to be humble as he views his limitations, yet the possibilities for smugness and for false pride are very great. He is easily tempted to regard his powers as equal to every occasion—yet reminders of his inadequacies make it impossible for him to rest easily in this delusion. He is tempted, especially if he looks upon himself as a wise scientist and a scholar, to regard the knowledge he has gained, and the theories he has brought forth, as final and conclusive—yet he can never escape from uneasy doubts. As his imagination soars and his powers of observation and reasoning are unleashed, he is tempted to conclude that he has found absolute truth—yet he can never fully avoid reminders that often he is fallible and foolish. When he contemplates what man's mind has accomplished, he is tempted to believe that if men would only use their reason and properly discipline their minds, they could achieve endless and unlimited progress and conquer pain and fear—yet he is reminded that men have often, in the name of truth and right, perpetrated cruelty and error.

Even when men make the most ambitious use of their capacities. then, they are faced with their own finitude; and the more towering their pretensions become, the more likely it is that such reminders will produce conflict and anxiety. Such conflict and anxiety are inevitable, for man is so constituted that he will put his faculties to use and seek even to transcend himself.

But anxiety such as the foregoing, which a person faces more or less openly and knowingly as an aspect of the uncertainty that goes with living, is not the most burdensome kind. People can learn to take these tensions more or less in stride. They will even seek experiences that involve conflict. As we have said, a person who seeks to live will actively move into situations that are likely to arouse anxiety. He will not welcome this anxiety, but neither will he try to run away from life in order to avoid it.

More disturbing in its painful consequences, more destructive in its effects on the growing personality, and more harmful in the effect it has on one's dealings with others is anxiety of less direct and more hidden origin. This is the kind of anxiety generated by unresolved problems of the past, which, in ways not fully recognized by the person himself, leave him unable to face the conditions of his life in a forthright and realistic way because he is at odds with himself. Such a condition prevails, for example, in a person who suffers from irrational guilt when heaven and earth have long since gladly forgiven him. Such a condition prevails when a person harbors illusions about himself that the realities of life threaten again and again to expose—when, for example, his work as a teacher appears to him to spring from a desire to advance knowledge but is actually a vehicle for competitive drives, or the expression of an insatiable need to gain recognition and to overcome a feeling that he is, really, not much good.

The anxiety that is most disturbing is that arising because of conflicts involving something false or devious, including precariously maintained pretenses concerning oneself and others. This kind of anxiety is especially burdensome because it is necessary to be so careful in keeping up the pretenses and in avoiding circumstances that might expose them. It is therefore necessary to avert one's eyes from the fact that the anxiety exists.

Much that goes on in education is a means of evading anxiety of this kind. To say this may sound harsh but is really a kindness, for although it is painful to face anxiety, it is even more painful to try endlessly to evade it or to pretend it does not exist.

We will have more to say concerning this and other specific aspects of anxiety. At a later point in this chapter we will deal more particularly with theories of anxiety and with differences between anxiety and fleeting episodes of fear, anger, and other emotions.

Anxiety as an Essential Concept in Education

The concept of anxiety has for a long time been regarded as important in psychopathology, psychiatry, psychoanalysis, and clinical psychology. It has also, in recent years, come to be regarded as a crucial concept in the practice of medicine and in the profession of nursing. Increasingly, theologians and clergymen are recognizing the importance of anxiety in the work of the pastor (42, 52).

The concept of anxiety should be regarded as a key concept in education as well. Anxiety is an important element in the personal lives of teachers, and it penetrates variously into the lives of all pupils. If in education we try to evade anxiety, we thereby try to evade the challenge of facing ourselves; we evade an essential task and make added trouble for ourselves and others.

The theory underlying this book is that to teach we must know the people we teach and the obstacles to learning (and teaching) that exist. To know the people we teach we must recognize that anxiety plays, or may be playing, an important role in their lives and in our own. The one who cannot learn is often an anxious child. The one who will not learn is often an anxious child. The rebel, the cut-up, the scatterbrain, the hostile child, the child who is aggressive and defiant—is often an anxious child. It is not only those who tremble who are anxious.

For a teacher to know those whom he teaches and their anxieties, he must know himself and seek to face his own anxieties. This, in brief, is the rationale for bringing the concept of anxiety into teacher education. Attention to this concept is at least as important in teacher preparation as the attention that has been given to academic aspects of educational psychology. In the writer's judgment, it is just as important as the attention that has been given to methods of teaching and supervision or to such subjects as the history and philosophy of education. Actually, these disciplines do not rule out the treatment of anxiety. The history of education, if studied in some depth, is in part a history of man's efforts to evade or to face anxiety. The philosophy of education, if it really cuts into the meaning of things, is in large measure an endeavor to face anxiety—especially the anxiety of meaninglessness and emptiness. Yet, as we know, history and philosophy can be taught in a way that is almost purely academic, with little or no attention to the personal implications of the human struggle.

The Nature and Some of the Conditions of Anxiety

Anxiety may arise as a reaction to anything that threatens one's existence as a separate self or that jeopardizes the attitudes one has concerning oneself and one's relations with others.

Anxiety occurs both as a response to a threat and as a way of alerting a person to evade or be on guard against anything that might threaten an irrational attitude or style of life he has adopted in trying to cope with the problems of his life.

Anxiety can be described as a state of distress, uneasiness, disorder, or disturbance arising from some kind of stress within the personality. The essential feature of this stress is that it is due, at least in part, to inner or subjective conditions as distinguished from external or objective threats and dangers. Where there is anxiety, there is some kind of threatening condition, dislocation, rift. disharmony, or inconsistency within the self. Such a condition prevails when a person is beset by conflict between opposing impulses and tendencies within himself—when, for example, there is a difference between what he is and what he pretends to be and his pretense is threatened in some way (he is eager to see himself as one who knows the answers, and then is reminded of his ignorance; or he is eager to see himself as a generous person, but feels uneasy because he is bitterly ungenerous toward those who question his generosity).

There is a state of anxiety when, for example, a person skillfully uses democratic techniques to ingratiate himself with others, or to manipulate them (possibly for ends that are very worthy), but cannot bear to face himself as an ordinary human being whose motives are rather mixed and include many very undemocratic leanings. There is anxiety when a person's insistence on rigorous scholarship happens to rest, in part, on a desire to dominate others, but he cannot bear openly to face this and needs to see himself, in spite of uneasy doubts now and then, as motivated only by an interest in scholarship.

There is anxiety when the aggressive people who habitually dominate educational meetings suspect (by the intensity of their impatience when other people are talking), but dare not face the thought, that they talk so much because of a compulsion to talk rather than because they have so much to contribute. There is anxiety, likewise, if those who do not talk, but would like to, feel tense and aggrieved but do nothing about it.

There is anxiety when a person who puts on a show of good fellowship as he dashes from one meeting, conference, party, or tea, to another, and who appears to be living a life that is full of companionship, now and then is disturbed by the deep current of loneliness that runs through his life.

There is anxiety when a person, claiming that teaching to him means everything, uneasily, once in a while, is confronted with the thought that his work does not satisfy all his needs and that perhaps something important is missing from his life.

These are only a few of the situations in which anxiety-producing conflicts may occur, and each of these situations represents, of course, only a surface manifestation of a deeper conflict.

Some Theories of Anxiety

Theories concerning the origin of anxiety have already been touched on. Prominent among these are the theories advanced by Freud (8), Horney (18, 19), and Sullivan (50). Other theoretical contributions have been made by May (38), Mowrer (in Hoch and Zubin [14]), and others. Tillich (52) has discussed conditions in human existence that underlie anxiety and has made an interesting distinction between anxiety as a psychological and as a philosophical and religious problem. Many of Kierkegaard's works of over a hundred years ago, notably the book entitled *The Sickness unto Death* (35), deal with anxiety as it appears in connection with a person's struggle for selfhood.

FREUDIAN THEORIES

Freud advanced several conjectures concerning anxiety. One of these related the origin of anxiety to separation from the mother in infancy. The concept of "separation anxiety" has many ramifications, and some features of it are touched on later in the discussion of loneliness. Freud's classic work on anxiety (8) deals with the phobia of horses exhibited by little Hans; underlying this phobia, according to Freud, was anxiety stemming from ambivalent attitudes toward his father —attitudes associated with an Oedipus complex.

29

HORNEY'S THEORY

In this chapter more space will be given to Horney's theory of anxiety than to any other. There are several aspects of anxiety that Horney's theory does not touch upon, and it leaves many questions unanswered (as do all accounts of anxiety, including the present one), but it has a merit that makes it especially meaningful in this book: there is something distinctly personal about it. A person who reads Horney's account of anxiety with an open mind cannot help recognizing characteristics within himself. Moreover, many of one's associates are reflected in one way or another in the mirror Horney holds up to human nature in her discussion of anxiety. The account that follows is abbreviated. The writer has taken certain liberties with the theory by applying it particularly to people in the educational profession. The theory applies to others equally well, of course.

Basic Anxiety and Attempted Solutions.—According to Horney's concept (18, 19), there is a kind of basic anxiety linked to a child's helplessness when he has to deal with a world that is hostile, unjust, and unaccepting and with an environment that blocks the free use of his energies and hinders his efforts to be himself. Conditions that interfere with the child's freedom to grow do not arise simply because his elders are malicious or harsh or wish to do him harm. They may occur partly because these persons are so absorbed in their own problems or in their own anxieties that even though they love the child as much as it is humanly possible for them to love him, they still do not have the inner freedom to notice, accept, and encourage him.

A child in such circumstances is thwarted and frustrated, but it is dangerous for him to show anger openly or to fight back. So he develops certain defenses and "strategies" in coping with his own inner response to the threats that are visited upon him from without. While these strategies may be the only measures he can possibly take at the moment and under the circumstances to protect himself against a forbidding environment, they may become so strongly entrenched that they function like acquired personality traits. Anxiety arises when these strategies are threatened, as happens when they conflict with reality or with one another.

Horney lists three major directions such strategies may take. She also indicates that they seldom appear in pure form; the same person may use different strategies in different circumstances. Nor are these ways of behaving, *in themselves*, signs of disturbance.

One strategy a person may develop in coping with an environment that thwarts his striving to become a person in his own right is to *move against*. Such a person becomes aggressive, expansive, and competitive. He seeks to control, to vie with others, to outdo or to rise above them. In the scholarly world, the strategy of aggressiveness may take the form of using scholarship as a medium for outdoing others. A person employing this strategy pursues learning not primarily because he is curious (although at times his curiosity will be strongly aroused), or has a practical need for knowing, but as a means of vying with others. One can find much apparent evidence of such a neurotic employment of scholarship at all academic levels.

Another strategy that may be used by a person who is thwarted in his striving for self-realization but is unable openly to oppose those who thwart him is to *move away*, to withdraw, to remain aloof and detached. A person using this strategy does not move freely and fully into the center of things with his feelings as well as his actions and his thoughts—now yielding, now resisting, now cooperating, now competing, free to like or dislike, to join or to go his own way according to the promptings of his own purposes and desires. Instead, he remains emotionally uninvolved. In the scholarly world, a person's bookishness may be a form of detachment when it is not something spontaneous or freely chosen but a means of side-stepping his conflicts. A detached teacher is one who, so to speak, teaches with his head but not with his heart. His thoughts flow freely but his feelings do not.

A person who has developed a strategy of detachment as a way of meeting life's problems is, emotionally, rather cold-blooded, although he is likely, sometimes, to give the opposite appearance. In the sphere of sex, for example, the detached person may go from one affair to another as though he were full of passion. But the sexual exploits of detached persons are actually rather pathetic and futile, involving no real emotional closeness with another person and little sharing of feeling. Although such people seem potent, they are, in a sense, emotionally impotent. When a person who has a capacity for entering into a deeply affectionate relationship with a member of the opposite sex reads or hears about the exploits of these detached people, he may be impressed. A person with a strong capacity for relatedness to others may actually have no talent at all for the fly-by-night affairs of the detached individual. He may even see himself as comparatively impotent until he recognizes that the detached individual, who seems so adequate, is a compulsive and probably also a very lonely and unhappy person.

A third strategy that may be developed by a child in an environment essentially hostile and thwarting is the strategy of *compliance*, *conformity*, *self-effacement*, and *appeasement*.

The compliant one moves with the tide, so to speak, instead of bucking it like the person who resorts to aggressiveness. He yields, instead of becoming a bystander like the one who uses the technique of detachment. In the educational world, the compliant one may meekly accept everyone else's verdict as to what he should learn or think. He may be so compliant that he gobbles up any and every kind of academic fodder. But this compliance is a means of self-protection, not a form of self-fulfillment.

Strategies such as the foregoing, undertaken as a means of protecting oneself, may appear in many forms and are likely to be mixed. The same person may use compliance as a maneuver in one situation, aloofness in another, and aggressiveness in yet another. But what is important is that these are expedients. To the extent that a person lives according to these strategies, he is playing an assumed role. He is denying himself, so to speak. The devious ways he has adopted are not enterprises reflecting his "real" self—enterprises he would undertake if he were free to use his resources and to draw on them in an unfettered manner.

When a person goes on to incorporate these strategies into his way of life as though they were an essential part of his nature—and not a driven endeavor to compete, to withdraw, or to appease—he has begun a process of alienation from himself.

The Idealized Image.—In order to support strategies such as the foregoing, according to the Horney theory, a person will resort to all kinds of additional expedients. He will use his powers of reasoning and imagination to convince himself that his strategies are an intrinsic part of his real nature. He may see his competitive striving for power as evidence that he possesses a kind of primitive strength in a world where one must bite or be bitten. When he succeeds in seeing himself in this light he is spared, at least for the moment, from painful awareness that his competitiveness has a compulsive quality—that it is not he who drives, for he is driven. He may see his compliance—his tendency to give in, to efface himself, to surrender his own rights and wishes and to calculate always what others want and wish—as a sign that he is a noble and generous person rather than one who is impelled to appease others in irrational ways. If he acts according to the strategy of detachment, he may see himself as one who is able to go it alone—a strong, reasonable individual with a lofty talent for disinterestedness and objectivity.

According to Horney, there is a tendency for strategies such as these to become integrated into what she calls the "idealized self." The idealized self is a kind of pseudo-identity through which a person gains a false rationale and integration of strategies and "solutions" he has been driven to adopt in his dealings with others. This idealized self differs from what might be called the real, or potential, self, which represents a person's actual resources for growth and self-fulfillment. Gershman (11) refers to this idealized self as the epitome of a person's defense system.

It is important to bear in mind that these "solutions" (which do not really resolve the problem) have a tendency to outlast the occasion that required them. A strategy of meekness, for example, may persist even after a person has become an adult and, when viewed objectively, is a strong person in his own right. Likewise, a tendency toward aloofness and detachment, or toward compulsive competitiveness, can become so strongly entrenched in childhood—as a conditioned personality trait, so to speak—that the person as a youth and as an adult retains the trait even though the external conditions of his life have changed and, objectively, there is no need for it any longer.

Anxiety as a Result of Discrepancy between Real and Ideal. —Anxiety comes into this picture, according to Horney, when a false system, which a person has built as a defense in an effort to compromise with life and in a desperate need to protect himself against hostile circumstances, is tampered with or threatened. Anxiety is aroused when a neurotic solution is threatened. It enters into the picture by virtue of discrepancies between the idealized image and the real self. There are many ways in which such threats may occur.

Anything that is false is, of course, precarious. There is the danger of being exposed—to oneself and also, incidentally, to others. There is also the possibility of collision if a person uses a mixture of incompatible strategies or if the promptings of the healthy part of his nature come into conflict with his unhealthy attempts at solution.

For example, a person who tries to cope with what he perceives as a predominantly hostile world by being meek, compliant, and self-effacing is bound now and then to feel a surge of revolt against this way of dealing with life. At times he will feel that he is being put upon, that others are taking advantage of his good nature. Instead of always enjoying a virtuous glow of subservience, he will have moments when he feels defiant. He may feel the beginnings of an upsurge of rage. But when he feels this way, he is likely to externalize his difficulty, to see himself as a victim of others rather than as a victim of his own compulsion to appease. He is likely to feel abused by others and fail to recognize that it is he himself who, in effect, has invited others to take advantage of his "good nature." But the upheaval of anger—even if brief, and even if directed outward—is still a very disquieting thing: it is incompatible with his view of himself as a charitable, long-suffering, compliant sort of person. So it involves, as indicated above, a threat to his idealized image of himself. It threatens to unmask and expose the picture of himself that he has so carefully cultivated. And this, according to the theory here under review, produces anxiety. The anxiety may be so horrible and terrifying to the appeaser that he plunges into the task of banishing any impulse to be defiant. He may resolve with desperate fervor to let his compliance—what he sees as the good part of his nature—take possession of him. We have in such a driven person a form of goodness that is demonic.

In like manner, the one who uses aggressiveness as a strategy and who has built an image of himself as an enterprising, energetic, strong person may suffer from misgivings that become threatening. A compulsion to compete and to achieve power over others is a very cruel kind of compulsion. A person who is driven to compete—which is different from competing in a zestful, spontaneous way—is in bondage. He is a slave. There are times when he would like to rebel against this slavery. There are times, too, when the promptings of compassion and friendliness, which are potential within every human being, clash with his aggressive need to move against people. This is threatening. When a person who struggles to hold a view of himself as someone who is hard suddenly is confronted with impulses within himself that are "soft," there is conflict. There is conflict between his idealized or assumed self and tendencies that belong to his potential self, and that might have been a part of his real self. So he becomes anxious.

The detached person is also bound, now and then, to meet with threats to his detachment. A young man or woman, for example, may be moved toward emotional closeness with a person of the opposite sex even though, as noted earlier, he or she may previously have entered into sexual relations in an unfeeling way. There is a danger of deep emotional involvement in this relationship. There is perhaps even the danger of falling in love. Now such an involvement, moving the person toward intimacy and tenderness and perhaps an all-out emotional attachment to another, is something very different from standing aloof and apart like an unconcerned spectator. So there is collision and conflict and anxiety.

To some people who have carefully cultivated a detached way of living, the threat of becoming intimately involved emotionally with another is so frightening that they resort to almost any means to ward off the threat. They may pretend that they really are incapable of feeling deeply about anyone. If their detachment is combined with a streak of aggressiveness, they may go to pains to tell the other person that he or she does not have what it takes to really stir up their feelings: he is not physically attractive enough, or has other faults and shortcomings. These shortcomings may be quite real—every person has his own brand of limitations—but they are used by the detached person as an afterthought, as a means of supporting the need to keep an emotional distance between himself and others—a need stemming from lack of emotional closeness to himself.

One can sometimes see a similar development in the relations between a pupil and a teacher at school. There are pupils who have cultivated an attitude of aloofness, seeming not to care about anything or anybody, who react with what seems almost a savage kind of hostility (for a time) when they come into the hands of a kindly teacher. Such a teacher threatens to release in them a wave of fellow-feeling, which they have sought to suppress.

The pose of being aloof, remote and removed from others

37

and from the mainstream of life, is a difficult one to maintain. The detached person, for all his seeming lack of feeling, is still a creature of emotion. Now and then he may feel a surge of anger toward someone (and being angry is definitely different from being uninvolved), or he may feel a surge of tenderness for someone (and one cannot have both a feeling of tenderness and a need for aloofness and feel comfortable about it). There are cracks in his armor through which a trickle—and perhaps even a flood—of emotion might enter. And this is threatening and produces anxiety.

The person whose detachment takes the form of moving, through scholarly pursuits, away from the personal into the impersonal, from the emotional into the intellectual, is also vulnerable. He suffers from anxiety when someone or something threatens to bring home to him that he is using his scholarly activities as a stratagem: he has taken flight from self into an ivory tower. One way people show the anxiety induced by this threat is to become enraged. And since the threat of exposure is so painful, they sometimes try to enclose themselves even more firmly within their academic tomb.

In the present study it was not possible to explore, in a systematic way, the theory that anxiety arises when something threatens a person's idealized image of himself, for to do so it would have been necessary to delve into the unrecognized or unconscious aspects of the idealized image. It was possible, however, to look into some of the recognized difficulties people have because of the demands and expectations they place upon themselves.

A large proportion of the people who were interviewed showed that they placed heavier demands upon themselves than they were able to meet. Many revealed a lack of confidence and assurance that they were worthy in their own right. This was shown, for example, by the need constantly to compare themselves with others and to assure themselves that they were better than others, or at least as good. Many indirectly expressed the demands they were placing upon themselves by complaining that *others* were demanding more than they could live up to. It is probably correct to assume that frequently, when people tell of the exorbitant demands others place upon them, they are attributing to others stern oughts and shoulds that they are imposing upon themselves. They are saying, indirectly, that they are not living up to an ideal of what they ought to be.

On the Personal Issues Inventory almost two thirds of the people in two groups, totaling 229 persons, identified a discrepancy between the real and the ideal—between themselves as they are and as they think they *ought* to be—as "one of the areas in which I probably need help in understanding myself."

This discussion does not imply that ideals are undesirable. They definitely are desirable when they fall within a healthy range. But the idealized image of self is unhealthy when a person, in striving to live up to an impossible expectation, devotes his energies to unrealistic aims and, in the process, fails to discover and neglects to develop his real strength. Also, by striving futilely to live up to an idealized image of self, a person may find it impossible to come to terms with the ordinary shortcomings he shares with all human beings.

SULLIVAN'S THEORY

Sullivan's theory of anxiety (50), like Horney's, takes into account the concept of the developing self and the child's dependence on others. The child's self develops in an interpersonal field in which there are persons who are significant to his life, growth, and well-being. Anxiety, according to Sullivan, has its roots in the disapproval of people who are significant in the child's interpersonal world. The attitudes of these significant people toward the child have a crucial bearing on his attitudes toward himself, for his self is made up of "reflected appraisals." The child's earliest appraisal of himself, according to Sullivan, is in terms of what others think and feel about him. If others think and feel about him in a derogatory way, the child's attitudes toward himself will be derogatory. The attitudes that prevail in the child's interpersonal relations become a part of the intrapersonal feature of his being and go into the making of what we call the self. When what Sullivan refers to as the "self-system" has been formed, anxiety may be aroused by anything that is alien to it or threatens it, even if the picture of self is a false and unhealthy one.

Anxiety and Fear

One way of clarifying the concept of anxiety is to distinguish between what is commonly known as *fear* and what may be described as *anxiety*.

In this section many such distinctions are drawn. Some of the differences outlined may, to some readers, seem controversial, and so they are. The purpose in listing them is not to insist that *this* is fear and *that* is anxiety, but to try to communicate some of the meanings and experiences related to both fear and anxiety. If something is described as fear that a certain reader might list as anxiety, the writer believes that this, in the present context, is not a serious shortcoming. The distinctions may help others to identify elements of their own experience or assist even the critic, through a negative process, in clarifying his own meanings. Moreover, even if one does not fully accept a given distinction, one can still recognize a difference. This point is labored here because one way of responding anxiously to the idea of anxiety is to resist it and to avoid its implications; and one form of resistance is to insist on a letter-perfect definition—to keep fiddling with meanings until the concept becomes only an academic matter and ceases to have any personal significance at all.

There are some rather specific criteria that help distinguish fear from anxiety.

One is the criterion of *objectivity-subjectivity*. Generally speaking, the threat in fear is objective, in the sense that there is an external danger that others would recognize as such. A snarling dog advances toward me, and I get scared. This is fear. On the other hand, an important element of the threat in anxiety is subjective. A person has a phobia of dogs, let us say—that is, all dogs touch off an irrational and unrealistic complex of inner disturbance, regardless of whether a particular dog is friendly or is held in a safe leash, etc. In this instance there is anxiety—the dog is not feared for its own sake, so to speak, but for what it symbolizes.

To state this distinction another way, fear is a response to a *danger from without* (this fellow is a mean guy and might hit, so I am afraid as long as the mean fellow is around); anxiety is a response to a *danger from within* (the presence of an unpleasant person touches off strong feelings of hostility, or even an impulse to murder, and these are more disturbing than the physical danger represented by the mean person).

Yet another distinction is that a person tends to be *discriminating* in his fears (although by no means perfectly so), while he is quite *undiscriminating* in his anxiety. For example, he is frightened, and for good reason, when he is criticized by a superior who has the power to fail him or demote him. On the other hand, if he has a deep need to be approved by everybody, he may be seriously disturbed by criticism from someone whose opinion really does not mean much from a practical point of view.

Generally speaking, the response in fear tends to be *proportionate* to the external stimulus, while in anxiety it is often quite *disproportionate*. After having been in contact with dangerous germs, a person is somewhat afraid and takes precautions until the danger of infection or incubation is past. But the anxious person may take elaborate precautions beyond that.

Usually fear is *"conscious"* in the sense that a person recognizes and perceives quite realistically what it is that scares him. Anxiety is *"unconscious"* in the sense that the decisive element in the distress is frequently not recognized for what it is.

As implied by the foregoing, there is a difference also in the duration of fear and anxiety. Fear tends to be *temporary;* it may last long and often recur, but when the objective danger is over, the fear usually subsides. Anxiety, on the other hand, tends to be *persistent;* the disquiet lingers even after the danger is past or the obvious physiological effects (such as occur in intense fright) have worn off.

Other differences, in general, are that fear tends to be *acute* and anxiety *chronic;* fear tends to be *specific*, anxiety *pervasive;* fear tends to be *localized*, anxiety not so; fear tends to be *fixed*, anxiety more *fluid*.

Perception, Feeling, and Impulse in Anxiety

Many rough distinctions between fear and anxiety can be made, but the meaning of anxiety is perhaps shown most clearly when it is viewed in terms of the three classic components commonly regarded as belonging to a typical emotional experience, namely, the *perceptual* component (perception of the exciting event); the affective, or *feeling*, component; and the *impulse* component (the tendency to fight, flee, move toward or against, etc.). The bodily (visceral and skeletal) changes that occur in emotion are not now the center of attention.

In anxiety these three components are less clear, less easily identifiable, and less specific than in what we usually look upon as fear or in any of the other classic "emotions."

PERCEPTION

In the typical instance of fear (as usually defined), we perceive what it is we are afraid of. In anxiety the perception is not so clear, and it may be utterly unclear and confused. An anxious person says, I feel low, guilty, depressed, uneasy, etc., but I don't know why. The perception of what it is that excites the emotion is fuzzy. There is no clear condition or object or circumstance to which he can attribute his uneasiness. He may feel uneasy and depressed and think that he can perceive, or partially perceive, what the disturbing event is (as when he fixes upon a symbol, such as a dog if he has a phobia of dogs; or projects his feelings, as an angry person does when he does not see himself as angry but attributes anger to someone else and then, so it seems to him, is angry because the other fellow has given him grounds for anger), but, as the phrasing of the examples indicates, the perception is faulty. What he perceives as the thing arousing his emotion is not really the "exciting event"—instead it is, so to speak, the trigger.

As an example of unclearness of perception we may cite

the anxious person who is disturbed by a little criticism or a mild show of disrespect. The circumstance that disturbs him so badly lies within him: it is because he is so sensitive, so uncertain, so on guard against rejection (and at the same time so eager to perceive it) that a little rebuff from others puts him in agony. There is, of course, an element of clear perception; someone actually did make the casual remark he perceives as *the* event that caused him such agony. But this explanation does not take account of the condition that caused him to become so deeply disturbed by it.

It would be possible to point to many examples of a faulty perceptual element in the anxieties of teachers and pupils. A teacher who is already uncertain of himself may see a little grimace as a sign of ridicule and feel deeply hurt. A pupil who is anxious may perceive a minor question as a major insult, and so on.

FEELING

The feeling component is also blurred or extremely varied in anxiety, in contrast with ordinary experiences of fear or anger or joy. *An important thing about the feeling element in anxiety is that an anxious person may not "feel" anxious at all, at least as far as he can discern:* he may, according to his own view, feel anything *but* anxious (unless or until he has acquired a good deal of insight into his own feelings). This does not mean, however, that there is absence of feeling.

One of the many feelings that betoken anxiety is a feeling of fear, although in the sphere of feeling, fear and anxiety are not necessarily made of the same psychological stuff. The fear experienced by the anxious person may be very intense (as when a person is disturbed by a phobia), and it may appear in any of a vast number of manifestations, ranging from terror, uncontrollable fright, and horror to apprehension, foreboding, uneasy anticipation, and the like.

One of the ways a person feels anxiety is through feelings of anger. The anger may range from a towering rage or a flaring of bad temper or a deep, dull, racking feeling of hatred to milder forms of annoyance, irritation, edginess, exasperation, and the like. The feelings that one has when one "loses one's temper" are among the prominent feelings connected with anxiety.

Losing one's temper, and the feeling of anger involved in it, often represents a "feeling" of anxiety although it is not usually recognized as such. When an anxious teacher loses his temper with a child, for example, there probably is some kind of blocking or thwarting that touches off the anger, but there is the added fact that more than an external thwarting is involved. Anger may flare because the inner expectations are so terrible, not because the provocation from outside is so great. A teacher striving to live up to an ideal of skill and patience quite beyond what anyone can achieve will be thwarted when pupils do not confirm the impossible demands he is placing on himself and, through himself, on them. A teacher who cannot forgive himself the weakness of making a mistake may fly into a temper when he makes an error or when a pupil makes a mistake that is neither serious nor malicious. Again, a teacher or parent who is in conflict with himself because he cannot accept his sexual impulses is likely to be anxious about behavior in others that appears to have a sexual meaning, but he may not feel anxious or even frightened at all; he may feel nothing but pure and righteous rage, having nothing to do with anxiety.

Anger is so often the feeling component in anxiety that it is perhaps as appropriate to link anxiety and anger as it is to link anxiety and fear. Sullivan (48, 50), among others, has described some of the many occasions when peevishness, annoyance, and outright anger are the feelings associated with a condition of anxiety. As a matter of fact, in many situations (perhaps in most) when a teacher or a student gets angry, it is more meaningful to ask, What is he anxious about? than simply to ask, What is he angry about? When we raise the question of anxiety, we recognize that the explanation for his anger cannot be found in what happened but in what the happening triggered off in him.

One of the many reasons anger is frequently associated with anxiety is that anger is a feeling one often has when one is at odds with oneself but manages to make it appear to oneself that someone else is to blame. As noted above, one way of evading the discomfort of anxiety one might experience from facing the fact that one is a hostile person is to project one's anger onto others, and then to feel angry with them. Examples of projected anger can often be found in connection with examinations or seminars. A person seeks to evade the pain of facing the discrepancy between his real performance and the performance he expected of himself by blaming the teacher for giving a stupid examination or for being unfair. He may feel anger toward a critic who touched on one of his weak spots and view him as dogmatic or diabolic. The anger springs from inner thwartings, but it is directed outward.

In most schools, examination time provides a field day for the activation of anxieties and for the marshaling of a vast array of feelings, anger prominent among them, that divert both the student and the teacher from the inner issues involved. It is interesting that the so-called "objective" type of examination often arouses much anxiety. In passing, it may be noted that an objective test is actually grounded on a subjective base: the particular bias the instructor has concerning *the* facts that must be remembered and *the* particular phrasing that is the only correct one.

Another feeling component of a state of anxiety is a feeling of being "blue" or depressed. This feeling may range from deep despondency and melancholy to milder forms of the blues. It may take the form of a longing or yearning—a hard-to-describe feeling that there is something lacking or missing, that a deep desire is unfulfilled. The experience of loneliness, discussed in Chapter Three, probably often represents a condition of anxiety.

Another phenomenon of feeling associated with anxiety is, anomalously, a curious *absence* of feeling. This is hard to define, but it may be expressed variously by such phrases as "I feel dead," "I feel numb inside," "I feel so empty."

Another indication of conflicts that involve anxiety appears in attitudes revealing inconsistent currents of feeling—for example, when a person expresses a very loving or generous attitude toward humanity but has hostile and condemning feelings toward large groups of human beings. The teacher who claims that he loves children but dislikes parents; or that he likes girls but dislikes boys, or vice versa; or that he likes bright children but shows in many ways a deep contempt for dull children; or that he likes teachers but not administrators; or that he likes Whites but not Negroes; or that he feels compassionate toward Gentiles but not Jews, and so on, is betraying an inconsistency of this kind.

It is inevitable that each person will be drawn more to some people than to others; any honest teacher will openly admit that there are some pupils in his class whom he likes better than others. But this is something quite different from a generalized feeling of active ill will toward others.

IMPULSE

It is through the impulses connected with anxiety that a person can often get the most revealing clues to anxiety in himself and in others.

The impulse in anxiety is often quite devious or obscure. It may even be the opposite of what seems appropriate.

In a condition of more or less uncomplicated emotional excitement, the impulse is usually fairly clear, if one stops to take note of it. When frightened, one has an impulse to flee; when angry, an impulse to attack; when joyful, an impulse to move toward and into the joy-producing situation and to prolong it. Where there is anxiety and it is experienced as anger or fear, these impulses to attack or to flee will also arise and be fairly clear; but they are, in a sense, secondary impulses, springing from impulses that are not so clear.

Inconsistency of Impulses.—The impulses associated with anxiety may be quite inconsistent, at least on the surface. For example, a person whose anxiety is related to an endeavor to live up to impossibly high competitive standards may at one time shun competition, then seek it; he may feel an impulse to exult when he wins, or feel deeply depressed; at the moment of his greatest triumph, an anxiously competitive person may have an overwhelming impulse to weep, or to flee, or to do something that will belie or destroy his victory. There is a confusion of impulses, just as there is a confusion of motives underlying the striving to live up to an external standard of worth such as is involved in compulsive competition.

A person whose anxiety is linked to his sexual desires may likewise behave in ways that are inconsistent. He may have an impulse to run when temptation threatens, but he may also have an impulse to go out and actively get in the way of temptation. He may have an impulse to punish those who do what he fears to do, but he may also have an impulse to admire and envy them; and he may go to great lengths to peep at them by reading about sexual exploits.

The complexity of impulses connected with anxiety is increased by the fact that the anxious person not only has impulses to act in several conflicting ways when his anxiety has actually been aroused; he also has an impulse to evade, escape, or blunt the impact of anxiety. In acting on this impulse, he may resort to an almost endless series of maneuvers. Many of these have the character of *compulsive* acts, acts a person is driven to do, regardless of whether they solve the problem or make it worse. In order to ameliorate his anxiety or to deaden its pain, he may resort to alcohol and drugs. Some persons acquire a knack for going to sleep when anxiety threatens or becomes acute. In others, conflicts that are anxiety-producing express themselves in the form of psychosomatic ailments.

Resistance.—Much that is done in response to an impulse to evade anxiety falls in the category of resistance. Resistance tied to anxiety is one of the most significant phenomena connected with learning, yet those who have been most concerned with the psychology of learning have taken little notice of it. Resistance of this sort may take the form of not learning (not noticing, not hearing, not catching the meaning, not trying, not going to a certain source, not remembering the assignment). A common form of resistance is to avoid contact with writings on subjects likely to arouse anxiety, or, while reading such writings, to carry on an active fire of criticism and rebuttal.

Another form of resistance is to avoid people whose ideas touch off one's anxieties.

Flight Reactions.—One impulse that arises in anxiety, as in fear, is to flee, but the anxious person does not do so in a way that would openly show he is in flight. One of the most common methods of flight from anxiety in education, and in the scholarly professions in general, is flight into words. If a threatening truth is glimpsed, ward it off by arguing, discussing, and so forth.

Another form of flight is to treat emotional problems as though they were logical problems. One way, for example, of resisting the emotional implications of anxiety is to spend so much time and effort in getting a precise, logically perfect definition of it that its personal meaning is lost. Another example of flight from emotion into logic, often encountered at home and at school, is the procedure of taking a child's arguments or complaints at face value, arguing his arguments on their own merits rather than seeking to examine the emotional meaning they have for him and for oneself. A child may say, for example, that he was not given his turn, or that he always gets the smallest helping, or that he is criticized where others are praised. Although he may be wrong on all counts, the feeling he has about it is the important thing. But to face this feeling—to face the fact that even though one is meticulously fair as a parent or as a teacher, there still may be something lacking, something withheld, as far as the emotional experiences of the child are concerned—can be very threatening. To evade the anxiety this threat might induce, we argue the issue on logical grounds and do not try to face the emotional meanings.

There are other ways of fleeing from emotional involvement in order to avoid anxiety. The person who is anxious because of irrational expectations or doubts regarding himself may try to avoid any close friendship, or love, or marriage, by constantly balancing one prospective friend or mate against another, seeking through a process of logical weighing and measuring to avoid any intimate emotional relationship.

A related form of flight is to dilute the personal meaning of what is threatening by carrying it into a discourse dealing with impersonal aspects. One way of avoiding the anxiety one might feel if one were to face the personal implications of the bitter hostility often shown by delinquents, for example, is to deal with delinquency primarily as a sociological problem. Another way of avoiding the personal implications of an emotional problem is to deal only with its mechanical aspects. After a class session, for example, in which many members had faced the problem of anxiety about as well as people can in class discussion, one of the students (who had not previously taken part) complained that the real problem was physiological and that the instructor should have spent the hour in dealing with bodily changes in emotion. Still another example, which the writer has frequently encountered, pertains to the concept of self-understanding: there are some who seem eagerly to accept the idea that self-understanding is important and then at once proceed to strip the idea of its potentially anxiety-producing personal implications by applying it to others rather than themselves.

In teaching and in all the learned professions it is a justifiable source of pride to be scientific in one's approach to things. But insistence on being scholarly and scientific can also serve as a defense against anxiety. This does not imply that the typical scientist or scholar or teacher is using his energies to evade his anxieties. But there are occasions when anxiety prompts scientific and other scholarly undertakings, just as it enters into other pursuits.

The study of psychology itself can be used as a means of

evading anxiety. This happens when a student of psychology clings to a theory or a set of facts as an academic device for evading personal issues. There probably is no system of psychology that has not sometimes served people as a protection against the anxiety of examining themselves.

Work as an Endeavor to Blunt or Avoid Anxiety.—One way of blunting or evading anxiety is to distract oneself by keeping busy. In the educational world (and in other spheres of life) work of a compulsive nature is one of the most widely used means of warding off or deadening anxiety. Work and more work can serve this end—work that others call over-work; work that makes one a drudge; work one takes on even though one's work basket is already full; work one does on the plea (to oneself) that it *must* be done, and on the plea that one's performance of this or that duty is not only important but indispensable; driving, restless, relentless work; any kind of work, as long as it is work that keeps one too busy to face oneself, may serve the purpose, functioning as a drug to blunt the impact of anxiety or to avoid its activation.

Of course, not all work is a form of evasion or blunting of anxiety. Nor is the work done under the spur of anxiety useless: it may be quite productive. And some of the work may be essential and inescapable, since a person who uses work as a narcotic gets himself so boxed in that a piece of work must indeed be done—he must give this report or practice this piece or study this lesson or meet this appointment or write this letter or the consequences may be serious—but the important thing, the thing that betokens anxiety, is that he got himself into that box in the first place.

The person who uses work as part of his own anxiety-evading or anxiety-blunting technique may also have a compulsion to drive others to work just for the sake of working, without giving them a chance to discover the kind of work through which they might be most useful or creative. The grievances teachers have about tasks that seem arbitrary and meaningless probably often stem from the compulsion of administrators to work and to assign work as a means of coping with their anxieties.

Anxiety in Childhood and Youth

In any class in school, picked at random, a great amount of anxiety prevails. There are children who are obviously anxious, showing in various forms of "problem" behavior that they are at odds with themselves. There are those who seem to be "blocked" in their learning; those who are frightened at trying themselves out, timid, afraid to express themselves, as though struggling against a barrier within themselves; those who are deeply hurt when anyone criticizes them mildly; those who overdo or underdo, or always strive desperately to please, or are endlessly restless and on the go, or are always on the defensive. There are those who seem nonchalant, behaving as though they care too little when actually they cannot bear the pain of caring too much.

There are those who constantly bring severe punishment upon themselves by their misbehavior, surliness, rebelliousness, and defiance. We cannot, of course, infer that every surly child is an anxious child, but we can infer anxiety—which means a state of disharmony and uneasiness in the child's relationship to himself—when, for instance, he repeatedly and for no apparent reason is surly or defiant or misbehaving in a way that is not at all suited to the occasion. We can infer anxiety if he is defiant, let us say, even toward those who would befriend him, or quick to take offense where none is intended, or if he misbehaves in a manner that obviously is not just a healthy kind of protest and self-assertion but is so out of proportion that it is futile and damaging to himself. When a child, as a matter of habit, seems to overreact, we can assume that he is not simply responding to a present situation but is meeting the present in a manner that has been distorted by painful experiences in the past.

Anxiety appears also in the many forms of so-called "nervous" behavior. It is shown by the nail-biters and by the children who are driven by a kind of uncontrollable restlessness, an excess or fever of activity.

There is anxiety in many of the forms of behavior generally considered polite and desirable. It appears in the child who is quick to deprecate himself, who criticizes himself unduly, who holds himself to a standard no one else would impose on him, who is frightened at the thought of being anything but perfect. Such a child's uneasiness stems from distortions within himself in the form of excessive expectations, oughts, and shoulds. When a child judges himself very harshly it is likely that there is a large gulf between what he is and does and achieves, on the one hand, and the ideal toward which he is reaching, on the other. The exorbitant demand he places on himself is an inward condition, but he is likely to externalize it, as though it were his parents, teachers, or peers who demanded so much.

The children who are anxious are not solely those who show fright. They are the children who are not responding to the demands of the moment in a realistic way or to the opportunities of the situation for what they are. Instead, they are responding in a way that shows they are driven by conflicting demands, expectations, grievances, and fears that are a carry-over from the past. The anxious ones are the young-

54

sters whose response to the objective situation is distorted by a response to their own subjective condition. The demands placed upon them by others are confused and obscured by the demands they make on themselves. They are unable to meet life and all it has to offer, or to say yes or no on the strength of healthy wishes of their own.

When a teacher faces a class of forty children, forty children are there in a physical sense, but psychologically there are many more. Each child brings to his present state the child (or children) he once was, the child he now is, and the child, perhaps the impossible child, he is striving to be.

If, as teachers, we could look upon a particular child from this point of view, we might discover a kind of multiplicity within him. We might see that although he seems quite composed, he harbors within him the character of a rejected child, who uses various strategies to avoid the hurt of rejection. He may live according to the inner protective devices of a child who has been abandoned and might be abandoned again. He may contain within himself, psychologically, the child who bases much of his life on the premise that he must be suspicious, guarded, cautious, careful in all his dealings with even the kindest people, because once in his life it was only by being defensive that he felt he could survive.

The ghosts of old hurts, the souls of agonies of an earlier day, live on in many of our children at school—and in the colleagues with whom we work, and in ourselves. And it is to the extent that each of us has the courage to look into the haunted house within himself where these ghosts reside that he can gain some insight into the way the lives of others are ravaged by anxiety.

The view that there may be, so to speak, other children who are all part of the child we actually see can be illustrated further. The child who seems so free to decide whether he will study or not study, be an obedient pupil or a trouble-maker, may not be free at all. His present attitudes may have a driven quality. If he rebels, this need not mean he chooses to rebel. His present rebellion may be a carry-over of rear-guard actions against real or imagined enemies belonging to his past. Sometimes the driven nature of his way of life is obvious, as when he over and over again does things that cause him pain. There are many children who do this, and there are many adults who oblige by punishing again and again these youngsters who are driven almost to destroy themselves.

The child who obviously sticks his chin out for a blow is probably no more troubled than the one who allows himself to be hurt again and again and carefully conceals it. A child who thus conceals things may, for example, be a youngster who, hours after, "kicks himself" for a little mistake he made, or winces in anguish at the thought of some little "foolish" thing he did or said, or blames himself for mistakes that no one else would hold against him, or puts himself on the rack of feeling rejected.

STUDIES OF CHILDREN'S PROBLEMS

Many studies of children, particularly at an early school age, show that in the typical class there are several youngsters who are obviously troubled and who exist as "problems" to themselves and to others.[2]

In a review of studies in this area Ullmann (54) pointed out that while not less than eight per cent of school children are

---

[2] Among the investigations in this area are studies by Rogers (45) and Ullmann (54). Other studies dealing in one way or another with emotional problems in childhood and adolescence have been reported by Havighurst (12), Symonds and Sherman (51), Powell (41), and Hertzman (13).

regarded as "maladjusted" by teachers, this figure is conservative (and, we might add, not very meaningful). There are many lines of evidence indicating that when teachers identify children who are problems or troublesome, they are revealing more concerning their own ideas of what a child should be like in his external behavior than concerning the emotional condition of the child. The classic study by Wickman (56) showed, for example, that teachers were likely, some years ago, to rate as "problems" children who were aggressive, disobedient, or destructive, while they tended to overlook the child whose affliction was not shown in aggressive ways.

Rogers (45) used a number of ratings and other means of detecting maladjustment, such as evidence of being rejected; truancy; school failure; reading disability; being a "misfit" academically, intellectually, or chronologically. Forty-eight per cent of the children in the fourth, fifth, and sixth grades in the population studied by Rogers could be labeled not well adjusted according to a combination of at least two of the criteria used. Nearly one eighth of the pupils in these three grades could be considered seriously maladjusted. Rogers pointed out that when a child is maladjusted according to four or more of the criteria used in his study, he is a person who has a long and often tragic history of unhappiness and unfortunate life circumstances.

One of many indications of anxiety in children appears in connection with their worries (26). Large numbers of children say, for example, that they worry over not passing tests (even though most of them will pass), over not being promoted (although most of them will be), and the like. When such a state of worry prevails, it betokens a condition of inner stress that may include self-doubt, feelings of self-

57

disparagement, and feelings of inadequacy quite out of keeping with reality.

Studies at the high school and junior high school levels indicate that many disturbances, such as inability to get along with others and a considerable amount of self-rejection, exist among youngsters in these grades. (See, for example, Fleege [4], Hertzman [13], and Spivack [47].)

What we are heading toward is the general conclusion, on empirical grounds, which has been stated earlier on theoretical grounds: Every child is to some extent an anxious child; but some children, we may assume, are more anxious than others.

EDUCATIONAL IMPLICATIONS

The observation that so many learners are anxious has a profound and pervasive significance. In the writer's opinion, there is no observation of more general import that can be made with respect to the nature of the educator's task. Unless he grasps the concept of anxiety and understands, at least in part, how it might affect the child's private life and influence the learning and teaching process, the teacher will be unaware of a crucial factor in his work.

To say that every child is an anxious child does not imply that he is therefore neurotic or that there is something inherently bad about being anxious. Nor does it imply that it is necessarily the teacher's fault or the school's fault or the fault of anyone in particular, and that if somehow we could be more clever many children would be converted from being anxious to not being anxious. No matter how clever people were, some anxiety would probably remain. But the burden of anxiety need not be so studiously ignored, nor is it necessary, in the name of education, to condone and encourage many of the conditions that aggravate it. Just as we encourage every effort to relieve physical pain, especially needless physical pain, so we should encourage every effort to relieve or ameliorate needless psychic pain in the form of anxiety.

Just as one cannot deal with physical pain unless one knows that it is there and is aware of its nature and the conditions under which it arises, so one cannot deal with psychic pain unless one faces the fact that it exists and seeks to become aware of the conditions underlying it. It is only by facing anxiety as it exists, as fully as we can, without putting a false gloss on the human struggle, that we can begin to deal realistically with the children we teach and with the nature of our own humanity.

Conflicting Views Concerning the Value of Anxiety.—At this point it is necessary to face the fact that people in education (and in psychology) differ quite sharply concerning the uses and values of anxiety. On the one hand there are those who take the view that anxiety, while painful, is really a good thing. Their arguments are about as follows: Anxiety provides an incentive to good habit formation; it is only because of anxiety that some children will behave, conform, toe the mark, and learn what they are supposed to learn; under the spur of anxiety, a student may learn more subject matter than he otherwise would; much of the productive work of the world has been done by anxious people. In emphasizing arguments of this sort, one educator, at a meeting where the writer was discussing anxiety, commented that what we need in education is more, not less, anxiety. There are others who take a quite different view of the matter.

Anxiety as a Spur to Activity.—Under certain circumstances, anxiety may be a spur to activity and learning, at least for the moment. Because of his anxiety, a person may be industrious, vigilant, careful to do what others expect (or not to get caught as a nonconformist). Because of his anxiety, he may have a compulsion to work incessantly (as was noted in an earlier section), and he may get a vast amount of work done. As one means of dealing with the conflicts underlying his anxiety, he may be highly competitive, and in the process outdo others in the volume of enterprises he undertakes; he may be a compliant conformist, and in his compliance he likewise may accomplish many things. As one of his devices for playing it safe, he may become a perfectionist and in that role achieve a degree of accuracy and meticulousness that is quite extraordinary; he may (in keeping with the Horney theory) resort to detachment, in his detachment taking refuge in an ivory tower and there turning out a large volume of scholarly work. Much of the work he performs may be productive and socially useful.

Anxiety in Relation to a Philosophy of Life.—The kind of motivation just described is essentially negative. The person who is motivated by his anxiety may learn a lot and do a lot, but he learns and performs as one who is driven, not as a free and spontaneous person who does the driving. It might be contended that this kind of motivation is good, or is the only basic motivation there is in life. It might also be contended that we should promote this kind of motivation in education and not do anything drastic to minimize it. This contention does not, however, in the writer's judgment, rest on the merits of anxiety as such. It rests on a broader premise, which amounts to a philosophy of life. This is a philosophy that views the achievements of life in quantitative terms, as though there were intrinsic value in learning a lot and doing a lot of things. It is also a philosophy that views life in negative terms, as though living consisted in seeking some relief from tensions, frustrations, hurts, and conflicts and as though, without such irritants, there would be no activity or striving.

There is a different philosophy: the philosophy that there is no value in the volume of what one knows or the quantity of what one does unless one is achieving some kind of self-fulfillment in the process of learning or doing. According to this view, it cannot be taken for granted that learning ten facts in history or ten theorems in geometry is ten times better, or even a little bit better, than learning one fact or one theorem. The living of a life, according to this view, consists not simply in coping with hurts and frustrations (which do, of course, occur); it involves also an onward sweep, a positive movement, an endeavor toward self-fulfillment, an impulse to grow. Life should not be regarded as simply a struggle against the road blocks a stubborn environment puts in the way, for it has an impetus of its own, a zeal and a striving to realize potentials with which it is endowed.

Anxiety as Waste.—If we adopt the premise that there is something positive in life that is worth striving for and worth seeking, and that this positive value is best expressed, in the life of the individual, through self-realization, it becomes apparent that we must regard most of the forms of anxiety described in this chapter as liabilities rather than assets. This premise is assumed in this chapter, and it is elaborated in later chapters. It is expressed especially in the chapter on the search for meaning, in which the view is set forth that the ultimate test of the significance of what we teach and learn is not the *amount* that is learned but the *personal implication* of what is learned. On this basis, we would not condone anxiety or encourage the conditions that produce anxiety. We certainly would not encourage conditions that drive people to spend their energy in keeping up the pseudo-solutions of competitiveness, compliance, and detachment, which were described earlier in this chapter. We would not encourage conditions that make it necessary for a person to pretend to be what he is not or that drive him to place impossible demands upon himself. We would see the inner conflicts, the dividedness within the self, the compulsions a person develops in his endeavors to evade or to blunt the impact of anxiety, as a form of waste, a form of self-defeat, not as beneficial either to the individual himself or to society.

Anxiety as a Barrier to Learning.—Even if, however, we take the position that the only task of the educator is to get people to learn academic subject matter, whether it has any personal meaning or not, we would still have to view anxiety as more of a hindrance than a help.

There is an increasing body of data indicating that many of the difficulties children and adults have in learning are not due to poor teaching methods or poor learning habits as such but spring from, or are related to, emotional problems. The work of Ephron (3), for example, illustrates dramatically, with a few cases, how crucial a part emotional disturbances may play in reading disability.

One of many recent studies touching on the relation between anxiety and academic failure is a study by Penty (40) of poor readers in high school. Among other things, Penty's study shows that while youngsters with a reading disability often drop out of school, it is possible for such youngsters, if they receive some psychological support from others, to stick it out and to maintain enough courage and hope to graduate from high school. In the process, many of them show great improvement in reading.

Even if our philosophy were to let children suffer, on the theory that it does them good, we still would have reason, simply on academic grounds and for utilitarian reasons, to face the problem of anxiety.

Teachers' Reactions to the
Personal Implications of Anxiety

One of the most impressive features of the work underlying this book was the response people made when the concept of anxiety was discussed. One would hardly suspect
anxiety of being a particularly popular subject for a lecture
or a class discussion. It is virtually impossible to talk about
anxiety, or to listen to a talk about anxiety, or to join in a
discussion of the meanings of anxiety without becoming somewhat anxious oneself. Unless a person has developed so strong
a defense against awareness of his own anxiety that he can
view the strain of the human struggle in a completely detached way, the subject of anxiety has a sharp emotional bite.
For this reason, the favorable reactions of members of class
groups in which anxiety was discussed were rather unex-
pected. The people in these groups who expressed themselves
expressed an overwhelming sentiment in favor of dealing with
the subject of anxiety. They expressed a desire to try to face
the implications of anxiety in their own lives. Many went out
of their way to say that the treatment of anxiety was one of
the most meaningful experiences they had had in their postgraduate work. When rating forms and direct requests for
written statements were used, a large number expressed themselves as strongly favoring consideration of anxiety as a central
issue in education. Some of the results obtained from questionnaires, evaluation slips, and the like are presented in
Appendix E.

Our evidence concerning the exact meaning a consideration
of anxiety has for graduate students in education, and the
value it might have for them, is limited. But certainly this
stands out: People who care to express themselves (and more

people in the groups in question expressed themselves on the subject of anxiety than on any other topic among the dozen or so that were considered) not only favor the idea of bringing anxiety out into the open for as full and frank a discussion as possible but are generally eager to have this done. Even though there is nothing pleasant, and much that is painful and threatening, about anxiety, they are far more comfortable in the thought of facing it than in the idea of continuing to avoid it.

Why, we might ask, was the sentiment of those who expressed an opinion so strongly in favor of facing the issue of anxiety? The writer hazards a personal interpretation, based in part on testimony such as that already cited, on bits of conversation with thirty or more of these people, on written comments, and on grapevine information concerning what the members of the classes were talking about among themselves. The interpretation is this: Facing the issue of anxiety meant, to them, a way of sharing a human situation with intimate personal meaning. The discussion of anxiety was a discussion of something that to them was *real*, even if painful. It was something that involved them personally, instead of telling them, as so many discussions in education do, how to do something to somebody else. It penetrated to some degree the wall of isolation that keeps people emotionally separate from one another.

Many said that they felt a strong surge of fellow-feeling when anxiety was discussed. Actually, of course, one cannot delve into the problem of anxiety in a meaningful way without feeling a current of compassion—a kind of compassion that flows out to others because it springs from compassion for oneself.

THREE

Loneliness

Almost all the people who were interviewed in this study spoke in one way or another of their loneliness. They spoke of feeling isolated and cut off from others. All of them, directly or indirectly, mentioned barriers that separated them from other people or separated other persons from them. In a sampling consisting of the first group of eighteen interviews, every person, according to two independent judges, expressed loneliness in one way or another. Almost half of the 229 people responding to the Personal Issues Inventory identified one or more conditions of loneliness as representing a problem in their lives which they probably needed help in facing.

Many of the people interviewed spoke directly of their loneliness, while others expressed loneliness indirectly yet poignantly. Some spoke of the artificial nature of many human relationships; of the remoteness between people, even people who are supposedly close associates; of the barriers of mistrust that keep people from expressing their feelings or revealing themselves; of the danger of showing oneself to others as one really is; of the danger of being hurt, or looked down on, or thought queer if one shows how one feels; of the need to keep up a posture and a pretense.

Conditions Contributing
to Loneliness

Many circumstances contribute to the loneliness and isolation of an adult. Prominent among these are conditions influencing his development during childhood years.

ALONENESS

One aspect of the child's growth as an independent individual is that he seeks and maintains a great deal of privacy. There are many reasons, and very healthy reasons, for reserving the right to keep his thoughts and feelings to himself. As he grows older, he is careful not to bare his naked self to everyone—nor does or can he completely bare it to anyone.

One indication of strength in a personality is that one can be alone, walk alone, think and feel alone. The further a maturing person goes toward choices, commitments, and convictions that to him are of ultimate significance, the more he is in a position where he stands alone—alone at least in the sense that he takes full responsibility for himself. The decisive vote in each mature person's life is a single vote, and it is the person himself who must cast it. Such aloneness is not in itself loneliness, but it may contribute to loneliness, for when each person keeps his thoughts to himself, the other does not quite know how to approach him, nor does he know what he might share with him. Each person becomes, in a sense, a little island unto himself.

As a person matures, he will also become increasingly aware of his aloneness, in the sense of differing from others in his tastes, interests, hopes, desires, and sentiments. Such conditions of being alone do not, however, necessarily mean that he is lonely, for he is, in a sense, in good company—in his own good company—when he is free to draw upon his resources and has the courage to be himself.

Different, however, is the state of being alone that arises because there is a rift within oneself or because there is something strange and alien in one's relation to others. This state we call *loneliness* rather than *aloneness* because it involves an element of sadness and often helplessness.

SUPPRESSION OF FEELING

There are strong cultural forces that bring about loneliness. Quite apart from inner needs connected with his own growth, there are many pressures in society and many circumstances in child-rearing at home and at school that lead the growing child to isolate himself and to keep himself at a distance from others—and eventually from himself. Anything that leads a child to think that it is not right for him to feel or to show his feelings to others contributes to the process by which he cuts himself off.

From an early age nearly all children are told not to cry, not to show that they are hurt or afraid, not to reveal that they are angry. This process goes on at home and, to an even greater extent, at school. Even at the preschool level it has been observed, for example, that children feel freer to cry at home than to shed tears in a nursery school. But the process of destroying the child's right to feel often goes on both at home and at school.

In the elementary school there is a great amount of suppression of feeling. Not many children, at least not many boys, feel free to cry or to show their fears, and it is often very dangerous for them to show their anger except by indirection. (It is probably not a coincidence that boys, who are under greater pressure to conceal their feelings, outnumber girls approximately four to one in showing various forms of "problem" behavior.)

In high school and college it is almost unthinkable for a person to show any feeling—except pleasure, perhaps, and anger, and those indirectly. In all his years as a student, the writer does not recall once seeing a teacher who wept in class. The teachers remained unmoved—and were supposed to remain unmoved—and probably would have been ridiculed by some anxious members of the class if they had been moved— even when the class was in contact with deep human feelings. In literature classes, for example, students and instructors study writings that recreate life's tragedy, tenderness, joy, and pain. There are writers who draw upon deep wells of compassion. There are some who write as though on pages wet with tears. It is true, of course, that a person can be deeply moved by such expressions of feeling without showing it visibly. He can be stirred by "thoughts that do often lie too deep for tears." But so often, in the literature class, these writings become just another assignment. There are objective tests (preferably multiple-choice) to measure what the student gets from the outpourings of these great minds and hearts, as though they were merely another set of academic facts.

We contribute to the growing child's isolation and loneliness whenever we, in effect, tell him that we do not wish to know how he feels. Yet there is much in the school life of both boys and girls that would make even the sturdiest child express intense emotion if the pressures against it were not so strong. In some schools, it is true, there is much gaiety and laughter, but painful emotions are often squelched. At the elementary school level, for example, millions of children feel the sting of failure, the lash of sarcasm, and the pain of rejection. There are thousands who, week after week, know the torture of helpless rage. If all these children, and others who encounter countless hurts—some deliberately and maliciously imposed, some that arise in the natural course of life's struggle—if all these were free to cry, as well they might, there would often be a flood of tears at school. But such signs of distress would be unseemly. It is better, for the sake of decency and order, to keep up a pretense that all is well. And by a strange irony, which persists in our culture from a more primitive time, it is more appropriate, if one is deeply moved, to show it through signs of anger (sarcastic laughter, for example) than through grief and affection. An outpouring of feeling would be frightening to teachers who have rigidly schooled themselves never ʳo let the hurts and tender emotions of their own lives show in public.

We ask that the child hold back his tears and swallow the lumps in his throat, swallow his rage and his fear and his pride. We ask compassionate teachers to do the same. To do this is like swallowing a sword. It can be done, but it is not easy; it takes long practice, and it leaves scars. If the school is in a "respectable" neighborhood, in which stolid parents in stolid homes aid and abet the school's policy of suppressing emotion and denying the child the right to feel—or the right to show that he feels—the policy will be quite successful. Everything will be in good order, and all the children will be fine except, of course, those for whom the ordeal is too great. These will include a rather large number of "emotionally disturbed children," children who conceal their feelings but harbor vengeful thoughts, children who nourish grievances that follow them into adult life, children who suffer from psychosomatic ailments or take refuge in dreams of glory tragically different from the reality of their lives. They will also include those who quietly join the multitude of people whose lives are lived in isolation from others and in alienation from themselves—people who have forfeited the freedom to feel, who cannot draw fully and wholeheartedly on their emotional capacities, who feel baffled and at a loss when others show their feelings.

Fifty-nine per cent of the group responding to the Personal Issues Inventory identified one or more problems related to freedom to feel as "one of the areas in which I probably need help in understanding myself."

REJECTION

Another condition that contributes to loneliness is created when children are judged predominantly by an impersonal standard of value and are not accepted for what they are. We repudiate the child as a creature worthy in his own right and set him apart from ourselves, as though we had no human kinship with him, when we judge him according to a competitive standard. We deny the child's right to respect and affection when we judge him (or, as far as he can tell, seem to judge him) primarily by the marks he gets. We repudiate many children at school when we applaud the one child in twenty or a hundred who wins the prize and pay little heed to all the rest. We cast a child out from emotional communion when we look only at the grade on his report card and have no concern, at least as far as he can tell, about how he feels, about whether it was through fear that he did poorly or whether his less than perfect performance at school springs from a feeling of being abused or a desire to rebel. So it is not surprising when we find that these children, some years later, as teachers in their twenties, thirties, forties, and fifties, express loneliness and say that they feel out of touch with others at school. Their experience of feeling out of touch has a long history.

BARRIERS BETWEEN TEACHERS

There is much in the school situation that cuts teachers off from one another. What goes on in the name of discussion, faculty meetings, committee meetings, and the like often does not bring people emotionally together but keeps them emotionally apart. Everything may be discussed solely on an intellectual and logical level. Even though there are individual teachers who try to break the ice, seeking to reach out to others and asking others to reach out to them, there usually are many who keep a nice distance.

One condition that expresses a teacher's loneliness and also contributes to it is that feelings, when they are allowed to show, are often projected feelings. Instead of openly revealing his feelings as his own, he imputes these feelings to others. This is especially noticeable in connection with anger, but it appears also in connection with fear, tenderness, and grief. Anger, as has been noted above, is one emotion that, curiously, often seems to be permissible; yet even anger quite commonly can be expressed only in a secondhand way. The teacher is not free to admit to himself, "I hate that child (or fellow-teacher, or parent, or principal, etc.)" and then proceed to face this feeling and what it means. Instead, it is usually necessary to avoid so blunt an encounter with his real feelings; he must first attribute ill will to others in order to justify his anger at them.

71

When a teacher feels angry, hurt, abused, spiteful, vengeful, unfairly treated, full of grievance, and the like, there are two facts that are important. One is that he feels this way; another is that this feeling is directed toward or against something or someone. In many respects the first of these facts is the more important, but it is usually the latter that is aired, with the result that the feeling becomes, in a sense, detached and impersonal. By a process of attributing a grievance to something or someone else (perhaps justifiably), the anger becomes lodged, so to speak, outside oneself, as though it were a thing apart and not an essential feature of oneself. Even in his anger, then, a person often keeps a lonely vigil, perhaps feeling a bit guilty, perhaps not daring to ask what the hidden meaning of his anger might be, keeping himself removed from the personal implications of his anger and keeping others removed from him.

If I am angry (whatever the reason and no matter how justifiably), an important fact is that it is *I* who feel anger. The anger is mine. It is something of me. It is an emotion in me that might provide a bridge (although not a particularly inviting one) between me and another person. It is also an emotion that, if I could confront its meaning, might serve as a bridge that brings me closer to understanding myself. But if, instead of coming forth candidly with my anger, I project it: gripe about the weather, events or characters in the day's political news, the principal, the size of classes, the parents, the community, etc., then it is not I who come with myself. I center attention on objective and external aspects of the situation and thereby immediately divorce myself even from my own anger and from any opportunity for sharing my anger (which means sharing something in me) with someone else.

72

FEAR AND STRANGENESS

Some features of loneliness go back to childhood fears and anxieties. One of the early fears shown by a child is the fear of being alone, or being left alone. In some of the writer's earlier studies (28) this fear was reported as quite common after the age of one or two years. The fear appears in various ways. It may appear in the tension shown by a child when his parents are out of sight for a moment when the family is on a walk, or when the child in the baby carriage on a shopping trip loses sight of his mother and sees only strange faces about him. It may appear also when the child goes to a doctor or a barber or is left for the first time in a hospital by himself.

This apprehension appears also in the form of a fear of separation and abandonment. Often it seems quite groundless, for it may arise in a child whose parents are near at hand and have no thought of actually leaving him. But there is still a certain element of reality when a young child is afraid of being left alone, for he is actually unable to fend for himself physically or psychologically. The fear of abandonment seems to be most conspicuous after a child has reached an age when he is aware to some degree not simply of his physical but also of his psychological dependence on others.

This early fear of being alone may contain the beginnings of a feeling of loneliness, a condition that exists when a person needs human contact but cannot find it, seeks emotional closeness to someone else but does not receive it. A person in this condition is out of psychological communication with other important people. A child so situated is like a stranger, helpless in an alien country.

Probably all children, at one time or another in their early lives, have had acute experiences of being strangers at home or at school or in the neighborhood. There is such a feeling of strangeness when a child is in a situation that is important to him and he feels out of touch, unable to count on the good will of others with whom his lot is thrown; when he feels distrust and perhaps even terror.

This is an aspect of loneliness that may have an especially important influence as the child moves on into adult years. The absence of secure and friendly anchorage in relations with others—which at first threatens to leave the child helpless in his loneliness through separateness from others—may have the effect eventually, if severe enough, of undermining his confidence in himself. So ultimately loneliness is not simply a condition that exists in a person's relations with other people; it is a condition that exists in his relation to himself.

Loneliness and Self-Alienation

There are people who are lonely because there is no one, or hardly anyone, to whom they can turn, with the exception perhaps of an odd person in the neighborhood or a pet with whom they can share some intimacy. But these are not among the loneliest people as long as they are able whole-heartedly to seek and enjoy the companionship of another creature. This creature need not be one who figures much in the scheme of things—he may be an aged person whom most others have cast off, or a child who has little influence, or someone who is maimed or crippled. It may even be a cat or a dog or a bird. As long as a person is able to maintain a wholehearted flow of feeling and has the capacity to go out to this other creature, he cannot be counted among the loneliest ones.

Even the person who happens to be physically alone, having no other creature near at hand to whom he can reach out in an intimate way, is not necessarily the loneliest among the lonely ones, for he may still turn to himself for company.

Who, then, is the loneliest one? It is the person who is not at home with his own thoughts, the one who is alien to his own feelings, the one who is a stranger to himself—he is the loneliest person of all. And a large proportion of the people who took part in this study seemed to realize this fact: that loneliness denotes not simply a lack in relations with others but also, perhaps primarily, a lack within oneself. They did not ask merely that a friend should come and relieve their solitude or that gay companions should divert them from their loneliness. They asked for help in understanding themselves.

Homelessness

Some of the most poignant expressions of loneliness are voiced through feelings of homelessness. Homelessness was one of the categories of experience that emerged from our conferences with individuals and was included in the Personal Issues Inventory. Over a third of the people who responded to this Inventory identified one or more conditions of homelessness as a personal issue they needed help in understanding.

In expressing the condition referred to here as homelessness, some said they had roots nowhere; some said they went from place to place without finding what they were seeking; some said that they felt at loose ends, without any sense of belonging, whether they were at work or on vacation, at home or on the job. Some said that while they had once had a home, in a physical and a psychological sense, they felt that they had lost this home and had not been able to find another.

The condition of homelessness, as here described, is an

expression of loneliness and also has much in common, psychologically, with many of the other conditions mentioned by the people in this study. When a person feels homeless, regardless of where he is or what job he holds, whether he is at work or at play, it may be inferred that he also faces the problem of meaninglessness. He is not absorbed by what he does. He does not find satisfying values in his activities or in his relations with others. It is as though he moved about in a world without light or substance. It is as though he dwelt in an empty house.

It is possible that a person feels homeless because he expects too much of himself or others (the condition identified as discrepancy between real and ideal). It is also likely that some of those who feel homeless are not able wholeheartedly to seize the emotional possibilities offered by the situations in which they find themselves (the condition identified as lack of freedom to feel).

The condition of homelessness is a kind of emptiness within the self. For this reason, its cure is not to build or rent or find a home in the physical sense. The keenest experience of homelessness may occur when a person is well housed and is dwelling with his family. One person in this study spoke of his feeling of homelessness as being most acute at the very times when the meaning of home should presumably be at its height—on a Christmas Eve, for example. Instead of feeling at home and experiencing the sentiments appropriate to the occasion, he sometimes was swept by an almost intolerable feeling of sadness. He attributed this feeling as an adult to unmet needs for affection as a child.

In another book (20) the writer described the condition of a child who was psychologically homeless even though, physically, he had a home and shared it with several brothers

and sisters. He was hungry for a kind of emotional acceptance and warmth his busy parents apparently were unable to
give. So he tried himself to fill the empty emotional space.
He constructed a whole imaginary family: father, mother,
and two children; and in his fancy he enjoyed with them
homelike intimacies his actual life did not afford. But even
though imagination is powerful, fantasy alone cannot provide a home for a homeless child. So the child gave up the
imaginary family and tried, as best he could, by other means,
to maintain a makeshift home. He became an excessively
"good" boy in his relations with his parents, seeking through
his virtue to avert disapproval and to win some acceptance.
He also went out to others, by being docile and helpful, to
win a bit of fatherliness from this man, a bit of motherliness
from that woman. Out of his condition of homelessness as
a child grew a state of homelessness which for a long time
afflicted him as an adult.

The state of being homeless is an inner state: the person
is not at home with himself. He is, in many ways, an aimless
one, a weary wanderer, who can find no place to rest and no
rock on which to build. Linked with his emptiness there
may be yearnings and longings and an awareness that something is lacking. He is, so to speak, seeking something he
never has found: "a stone, a leaf, an unfound door." If such
a homeless one would find a home, he must first find himself
—he must learn to be at home with himself. This is not an
easy undertaking for one who feels homeless. But many of
the people who took part in this study seemed to recognize
that this might be the real issue when they recorded that to
face their feelings of homelessness they needed help in understanding themselves.

FOUR

The Search
for Meaning

In the first chapter the problem of meaninglessness was introduced as one that faces teachers and all other thinking people of the present day. The search for meaning is a theme that runs through all chapters of this book, just as the problem of meaninglessness arose in most of the interviews and in a large proportion of the written statements in this study. The search for meaning is essentially a search for self. Meaning constitutes, in many respects, the substance of the self.

Where there is meaning, there is involvement. When something has meaning, one is committed to it. Where there is meaning, there is conviction. Such commitment and conviction is something different from conformity, or merely playing a part, or living as a cog in a machine, or losing one's individuality in what Kierkegaard has called the "featureless crowd." Where meaning is lacking in one's work as a teacher, the self is uninvolved. The substance is lacking, and teaching is just an empty formality.

The problem of meaninglessness overlaps in many ways the problems of anxiety and loneliness. It is largely by virtue of a lack of meaning—a kind of emotional emptiness that prevails when things don't matter—that the lonely person feels lonely. It is partly because of a lack of meaning or a distortion of meaning such as is found in pretenses and inner disharmonies that the anxious person is anxious.

About sixty per cent of the people responding to the Personal Issues Inventory indicated that meaninglessness was a problem on which they would like to have help in understanding themselves. In expressing this problem, many said they were not sure what they wanted from life—what it was important to be or do or get from life; some said that what they were doing or what was happening didn't seem to mean much; some said they saw little or no meaning in many of the things they had to learn or teach. Some expressed meaninglessness by default, so to speak, indicating that they got involved in so many activities and responsibilities that they had little time for themselves.

The need for helping children and grown men and women to face and find something essentially meaningful glares at us from headlines telling of tensions in the world we live in. Man has made fabulous progress in exploring the external dimensions of his world and in controlling its physical properties, but this power has not been matched by a cultivation of his courage to draw upon other resources of his humanity. We are frightened lest he use his power to destroy himself. Modern man, for all his contrivances, is still as much in need of finding himself and facing the meaning of his existence as he was many eras ago. No invention in science or gimmick in education can obviate the necessity for this search.

The problem of meaninglessness—which Tillich has referred to as the anxiety of emptiness and the anxiety of meaninglessness—prevails not simply among teachers and their captive pupils. Meaninglessness is a common condition in college and graduate teaching. Much of what goes on in the name of learning is simply an academic enterprise. Even religion, as has been pointed out earlier, can be pursued in a meaningless way.

Education and the Search
for Meaning

The crucial test in the search for meaning in education is the *personal implication* of what we learn and teach. In some educational circles this will sound strange, for it often seems to be assumed that a body of information is in itself meaningful.

If we as educators are to face the problem of meaninglessness, we must make an effort to conduct education in depth —to move toward something that is personally significant beyond the facade of facts, subject matter, logic, and reason behind which human motives and a person's real struggles and strivings are often concealed. This does not mean the rejection of subject matter—far from it—but it does mean helping the learner to relate himself to what he is learning and to fit what he learns into the fabric of his life in a meaningful way.

Such an endeavor means an effort to overcome the prevailing tendency in education to encourage the learner to understand everything except himself.

It means an effort to achieve a better integration of thinking and feeling on the part of both children and adults.

It means an effort to cut through the pretense of "interest" in learning, which children and adults so widely adopt in order to conform or to escape disapproval from their elders. It means also that the process of learning will not be used as a means of competing with others and gaining power over them.

Actually, each subject that is taught in elementary or high school or college could, in one way or another, for certain learners, be deeply charged with meaning. Each subject could, in one way or another, help some young person discover his skills and explore or use his resources.

The study of history, to give only one example, can be an intensely meaningful experience, for history is filled with the substance of human hopes and fears: man's struggles, his pride, his shame, his courage, his joy. Much of history—perhaps all—can be taught in such a way that there is a direct line of emotional and intellectual communication from historical characters and actions to the intimate personal lives of the learners.

The same is true with respect to literature and all other academic subjects. It is certainly true with respect to physical education and all the arts, skills, and crafts, for each of these enterprises can be undertaken in a manner that has a direct and immediate personal implication.

But instead, much of what teachers have to learn, much of what they have to teach, and much of what the millions of pupils who attend our schools are compelled to study is not meaningful but meaningless, largely because we have assumed that knowledge has value apart from its meaning for the one who acquires it. When we consider the problem of meaninglessness, it is not extreme to say that one of the basic troubles in education is that as educators we have not had the courage to face the personal implications of our calling.

Helping Others
through Facing Oneself

To help a pupil to have meaningful experiences, a teacher must know the pupil as a person. This means, as has been repeatedly emphasized in this book, that the teacher must strive to know himself.

In the school there are countless opportunities for helping the child in his search to find himself. He can be helped to discover his aptitudes and abilities, to face some of his inner difficulties, and to realize his limits. What the teacher does strongly affects the pupil's attitudes regarding his worth as a person since, as has been noted, life at school is heavily invested with praise and blame, pride and shame, acceptance and rejection, success and failure. Everything in the relation between a teacher and a student has or might have a significant effect on what a child thinks and feels about himself.

To have insight into the child's strivings and the problems he faces, the teacher must strive to face the same problems within his own life. These problems are largely emotional in nature.

To be able to understand and sympathize with a child who is hostile (and all children are, more or less), the teacher must face his own hostile tendencies and try to accept the implications of his anger as it occurs, say, in his annoyance with his pupils, in his impatience with himself, and in his feuds with other teachers.

He must seek to understand the devices he uses to avoid responsibility for himself by blaming others.

To appreciate another's fears, a person must try to examine his own fears. He must face them as they appear in his phobias, squeamishness, fear of misfortune, timidity, uncertainties, unwillingness to take a chance, worry concerning what others may think of him.

Unless a teacher can, at least to some extent, face his own anxiety, he will be uncomprehending when children helplessly express theirs. He may be harsh when children's anxieties break through in such signs as inability to learn, impertinence, inattentiveness, restlessness, irritability, and the like.

A teacher's understanding of others can be only as deep as the wisdom he possesses when he looks inward upon himself. The more genuinely he seeks to face the problems of his own life, the more he will be able to realize his kinship with others, whether they are younger or older, like him or unlike him in education, wealth, religion, or professional rank.

How does one achieve understanding of self?

One broad principle is this: *To gain in knowledge of self, one must have the courage to seek it and the humility to accept what one may find.* If one has such courage and such humility, one can seek professional help and one can draw on many resources in everyday life.

One can learn from experience of life's joys and tragedies. One can profit from trying to catch the meaning of one's anger, joy, depression, fear, desire to inflict pain, and so forth.

A valuable help in self-examination, which may be mainly intellectual but may also strike at a deep emotional level, is the reading of books written by compassionate people who have made some progress in their own painful struggle to know themselves.

The method of "participant observation" offers one means of taking a look at oneself. One records what one hears and sees and what one's feelings are as one listens in on a discussion or visits a class. Then, with the help of others, one examines this record and compares it with records kept by other observers. This comparison may show how what one notices is determined by habits of thought that are taken for granted. What one perceives "objectively" is often a projection of one's own subjective state, and thus may tell more about oneself than about the people one observes.

This broad principle also holds: *Just as it is within an interpersonal setting that one acquires most of the attitudes involved in one's view of oneself, so it is likely that only in an interpersonal setting can a person be helped to come to grips with some of the meanings of these attitudes.*

A relationship that can promote knowledge of self prevails when one seeks private therapy or joins with others in a group therapy situation.[1] It exists also, to some degree, whenever one enters into relationship with people in any walk of life who can help one gain perspective on oneself. In a group, a person may be helped to see his anger, fear, and protective devices as others see them. The way others express themselves

---

[1] In an earlier study (27) in this series, a workshop consisting of teachers of psychology in the high school recommended that *all* high school teachers (not just psychology teachers) should be provided with such opportunities to grow in self-understanding as might be obtained through group therapy under the leadership of people professionally trained for such work. Such a proposal would involve many practical considerations that will not be discussed here, and it might not be an adequate solution for some people. It is mentioned here, however, to emphasize the point that many teachers recognize the need for help if they are to make full use of their personal and professional potentialities. As indicated in the first chapter, over forty per cent of the people in a majority of the groups answering the questionnaire on self-understanding stated that they thought they would need personal help such as might be gotten from group therapy if they were to put the concept of self-understanding (which over ninety per cent endorsed) into practice in their professional work.

or respond to him may help him perceive in a new and self-revealing light some of the evidences of shame, self-effacement, anxiety, vindictiveness, and other outcroppings of deep-seated attitudes of which ordinarily he is not aware. Similarly, to witness a mimicking of his conduct by a child or by a role-playing peer may throw some light on unrecognized conflicts.

Some of the richest possibilities for self-examination can be found in relationships with others from month to month and from year to year. In the teaching profession we have hardly begun to explore and to tap these resources for growth in self-knowledge, although some work is being done in this area. If people could encourage one another to come out from behind the curtain that commonly conceals their emotions from others and from themselves, these emotions might be faced in an insight-producing way.

In a larger sense, particular procedures that are used for growing in self-understanding are less important than the courage to face this need. Self-knowledge can be acquired in many ways. It is not something that is attained once and for all. Those who are blind to themselves have a little of it, and a capacity to acquire more; and an outstanding mark of those who have acquired the deepest knowledge is that they still are seeking. No one procedure alone will give the answer, since the search for selfhood, when genuine, is pursued through all channels of experience as long as a person lives.

FACING THE ROLE
OF FEELING IN THINKING

In the foregoing section the emphasis has been on the need for facing our own emotions if we are to make any progress in understanding the emotions of others. But there is a need for facing emotion also in dealing with what, on the surface, may seem to be the purely intellectual and academic aspects of the school's program. Much of what is called thinking is actually governed by undisclosed feelings. Logic is often ruled by desire; intellectual arguments are often the instruments of fear or anger. To the extent that this is true, the full meaning of what seems to be an intellectual discourse is not revealed or shared. To think straight, to communicate what we are thinking, and to think effectively about what someone else is trying to communicate, it is important to know how we feel, and how feeling influences our thoughts and the thoughts of others. It is necessary to take account of emotional factors in thinking if the intellect is to be given a chance to function freely.

We let our feelings govern the nature of our reasoning, without knowing that we are doing so, when we project our own bias onto a discussion of a historical issue, or a problem of discipline or scholarship, or a decision as to what courses a high school student *must* take to be allowed to go to college, etc., without once asking ourselves: Is this really pure reasoning, or am I perhaps projecting my own prejudices or yielding in meek but compulsive compliance to what others have demanded?

During the presidential campaign of 1952 a forum was held whose avowed purpose was to try to inquire beneath the reasons people usually gave to others and to themselves for supporting one candidate or opposing another. The members of the forum were instructors and graduate students. It soon became apparent that it was very difficult for these people even to ask themselves: Is there *perhaps* an emotional reason, apart from the logical reasons I give, for my support of one candidate or bitter opposition to another? What, on an *emotional* level, does this campaign mean, and what do the candidates symbolize in my own emotional life? How do I *feel* toward the personalities, parties, and issues, as distinguished from what I believe I *think* about them? The venture was a failure. The hour was spent in a rehash of the hackneyed arguments used in the campaign materials of both parties.

Someone might say that to ask people in education even to consider that there might be an emotional bias in the reasoning they use to support a political candidate is simply asking too much of human nature. Maybe it is. But unless we at least try to understand the role of feeling in our thinking, we are simply going through the motions of thinking. We are not making full use of our capacity to reason.

FACING THE PERSONAL
IMPLICATIONS OF IDEAS

One complaint often made by teachers in training is that they have to learn a lot of theory without being shown how to put the theory into practice. This is a problem, but it is probably not the basic problem. The problem may be that teachers are resisting the meaning of the theory as it applies to themselves. Any theory in education that has its roots in the realities of life has an immediate practical meaning to those who are willing to accept it.

Often, when teachers look for a practical application—a method, a gimmick, a prescription, a rule of thumb—they are trying not to grasp but to avoid the meaning a theory might have for them. Theory and practice are often out of gear in education because as teachers—like all other human beings—we like to externalize rather than internalize a theory. Our immediate response often is to become manipulative: to do something to someone else.

The writer has faced this problem repeatedly in his work

with the concept underlying this book: that an essential function of education is to help the growing child understand himself and develop healthy attitudes of self-acceptance. In some classroom situations dealing with self-understanding which the writer has had an opportunity to observe, teachers have done almost everything except the one thing that is needful. They have gotten long check lists of children's interests. They have talked to parents about the pupils. They have gotten the young people to express by a vote what to them seemed to be their most urgent and important problems. They have supplied movies and exhibits and have used all kinds of paraphernalia. But in doing all this, they often seemed to leave out the one essential thing: their own direct, personal involvement.

Hopelessness and Despair

Many people interviewed in connection with this study expressed themselves as rather hopeless of ever finding a solution for some problem or problems in their lives. In no instance, however, was there a consistent or pure attitude of hopelessness. The people who said or implied that they were without hope with respect to a particular difficulty also showed they still had a lot of courage left.

The concept of hopelessness was also included in the Personal Issues Inventory. Over a third of those responding indicated that one or more of the conditions of hopelessness described in the Inventory represented a problem in their own lives.

What we treated as hopelessness was expressed by statements such as the following: "I feel that there are important things in life I have missed and never will find, no matter how hard I try or how much I accomplish; I feel that there are things in life I have had to give up, and I suspect that at my age it is too late to make up for them; Although I believe life's struggle may be worth while, it often seems rather hopeless; I sometimes feel that life is so complicated and mixed up that I wonder whether it is worth while to keep up the struggle." There is a note of hopelessness in all these statements, and it is true that a person who shares the feelings expressed by them probably faces a large area of emptiness in his life. But there is a more terrible condition of emptiness—the condition of despair.

The utmost condition of meaninglessness in life is a state of despair. Where there is awareness of hopelessness, there is an awareness of what might be, and this in itself contains a ray of hope. There is still a possibility, as the Prophet has said, that the well of pain might yet be filled with joy. In a state of despair the prospect is bleaker than this. To despair is to surrender. The one who completely despairs has given up the quest for meaning. He has given up the struggle to be himself or to find himself. Despair is like death, but it is deeper than death. It is a kind of living death. It is what Kierkegaard has called "the sickness unto death."

Death is not in itself a symbol of despair. The prospect of death is a recurring theme in the history of a life in which there is still a surge of growth. Death can never be denied. But the one who is still in search of selfhood faces death and incorporates the thought of it into the larger sweep of his existence. He may go even further and accept death as something swallowed up in life. He may believe, or try to believe, that his identity lives on even after death—a belief that many hold but others deny. He may believe, as some have sought to believe, that he will live on in the memory of those who remain. He may believe that somehow he will survive even though his bones have been interred. He may believe, as some have endeavored to believe, that he can find eternal life, not through timeless existence, but through fullness of existence. According to this belief, a self that plunges deeply and fully into the possibilities of living captures and embraces the essence of immortality, whether or not the spirit survives the body. These are some of the ways of accepting or seeking to accept the threat of death and the inescapable fact that death will occur.

As was stated earlier, he who accepts himself fully accepts himself as one who will die. He who is best able to live is best prepared to die. He is one who, though facing the prospect of dying, still lives. In a state of despair, it is otherwise. For the one who despairs, if his despair is complete, has died while he is still alive. His is a living death.

Who are these despairing ones? The despairing ones, according to the view presented here, are not those who, in this study, spoke of areas of meaninglessness in their lives, or said they felt lonely or homeless or hopeless. These people are still alive in the search for selfhood. They have the courage, and the humility, to accept the fact that there is something empty in their lives. They say that there is something of deadness in their existence, but by virtue of facing this condition they are among those who are most alive. The despairing ones are not found among those who have the courage to face their anxiety, hostility, loneliness, and search for meaning, as did the people in this study who openly affirmed that they needed help and courageously asked for it. The despairing ones are more likely to be among those who pretend to be well adjusted and claim to be above ordinary human frailty. Their "adjustment" may be a form of despair: Adjustment to conformity. Adjustment by way of surrender of feeling. Adjustment to a condition of not even daring to face the issues of anxiety and meaning. Adjustment gained at the price of not daring to ask the question: Who and what and why am I?

There is doubt and fear and perhaps an element of hopelessness when one says, "I *don't* know what *really* matters." But there is something deeper than this—there is despair—when a person says, in effect, "Nothing matters." A person despairs when he renounces the most intimate possessions of humanity—feeling, passion, meaning, and choice. He expresses despair when he says that existence is simply a mechanical link in a chain of cause and effect, one event in an endless succession of antecedents and consequents, and that the search for meaning and value, or even the notion of the uniqueness of humanity itself, is just an illusion.

It is good to feel sympathy for those who weep, but more in need of sympathy are those who despairingly have surrendered the right to weep. It is good to go out in fellow-feeling to those who feel lonely, but more in need of fellow-feeling are those despairing ones who do not dare to face their loneliness or hope for anything else. One's heart goes out to those who say their lives are empty, but more deeply in need of compassion are those who say that life itself is empty.

The Paradox of Meaninglessness

When people feel that meaninglessness is a problem in their own lives—as so many in this study did—they express a kind of despondency. But there is a paradox in this despondency, for it expresses both an awareness of emptiness and an undercurrent of hope. There is hope because concern with meaninglessness in itself implies the possibility that meaning might be found. If a person did not have some hope, he would not ask for help—he would give up in despair. Where there is a desire to seek for meaning, there remains some assurance that life has, or might have, meaning. Most teachers who raise the problem of meaning probably have an unspoken faith that life has some worth, and an unvoiced conviction that their existence might have a significance richer than anything they have yet discovered.

This hope, which persists in spite of disappointment, has roots deep in the soil of life's early experiences. One outstanding characteristic of the young child is that he actively seeks to understand. In his first explorations, at first wordlessly and then through language, he seeks to examine, to probe into the what, the how, and the why. Even at an early stage of life he strives as though he had implicit faith that there *is* a how, a what, a why. Early in his strivings, likewise, he proceeds as though it were possible to get and to give an accounting of things. A remnant of this hope persists even though the child is often rebuked when, in school, he seeks to grasp the significance, for him, of the vast body of academic material he is compelled to learn. This hope persists in the teachers who took part in this study, even when, by their own testimony, they see so much that is empty and meaningless in what they are compelled to teach.

Granting that this hope persists, it remains true that many people who were interviewed and many who responded to questionnaires in this study revealed deep suffering when they testified that there were areas of emptiness and meaninglessness in their lives; that they tried helplessly to live up to impossible expectations; that they were not in touch with their real feelings. There is pain and probably often an element

92

of tragedy when people say, as did a goodly number in this study, that they feel lonely, homeless, and hopeless.

If a limited encounter with the idea of self-discovery elicits so much awareness of lack, meaninglessness, and loneliness, and so many evidences of disquiet, would not the picture become even gloomier if these people launched into a further and deeper search into themselves? The answer is Yes. And would it not be better to avoid this, to leave untouched these longings and yearnings, to leave uncovered these undercurrents of tragedy? The answer is No.

It is true that often, as a person inquires into the meaning of his life, he is likely to feel uncomfortable. He will find that he has been pretending. He will face feelings that are disturbing and depressing. But these conditions were there before he started to inquire. To feel actively disturbed by them can be the beginning of a process of repair and growth. And as long as the conditions are there, even if hidden, they mean trouble, even if the trouble is not directly perceived and is experienced through states of restlessness or aimlessness or vague apprehension, depression, boredom, anger, or frustration, such as were discussed in the chapter on anxiety. When there are dislocations in one's life, one pays a price somehow. The problems that are faced when one looks at these are old and troublesome, even if they seem utterly new.

The search for meaning—the search for selfhood—is painful, and although it is healing, the person who undertakes it is likely to feel worse before he feels better. It is only by accepting oneself as one is—having the courage to perceive and the humility to appreciate and to savor one's loneliness and hostility and the meaninglessness of so much of what one does— that the process of healing and repair can get under way.

The position in this book is that we should face the question of meaning in education, not evade or avoid it, even if it hurts. This is a position on which not all will agree. The writer has been told by some people that education should not enter into this area. We should not touch upon issues that might arouse anxiety. We should not press into the deeper areas of meaning lest the student become distressed. We should not even discuss anxiety (so a few have said), for to do so might make people more anxious than they already are. Yet what is the alternative? Actually, there is nothing significant that we can undertake at any level in education that will not arouse anxiety in some students.

As has already been noted, in the most conventionally oriented and psychologically naive learning situations, children face failure, ridicule, and rejection on a monumental scale. They constantly face conditions that create anxiety or aggravate that which already prevails. So to center our attention only on the academic, and to avoid any emphasis on what has implications for the self, will not rule out anxiety, even though it might rule out some occasions for anxiety. We do not avoid the actuality of anxiety by ignoring it or by refusing to look at life as it is. The only way to sidestep anxiety in education completely is to stop educating children altogether.

But, even apart from this, what is the alternative?

Should we, in order to avoid the risk of stirring people up, proceed in our pedagogy as though we were dealing in a mechanical way with disembodied facts? Should the teacher of English, for example, in sharing a poem or a novel filled with hate or passion or tears, avoid these emotions because they might evoke a resonance of feeling in this or that member of the class? Should he blunt the impact, strip out the passion, dry up the tears? Should he water things down so that no one will feel anything? If the answer is Yes, then why teach poetry, drama, or fiction? If No, then why not try for the fullest impact and the deepest possible significance?

The same question can be raised concerning everything we teach—every subject, every skill, every art, every craft that is part of the curriculum.

But the question, What is the alternative?, becomes even more insistent when we look at the children we teach. If we look at them realistically, we see that their lives, like the lives of teachers, are touched by anxiety, hostility, loneliness, guilt, and many other conditions of distress. If we are to face these children as they are, we must face the conditions as realistically as we can.

Religion

Many of the people interviewed in connection with this study spoke of religion. Some spoke in a mood of charity; some voiced bitterness and hostility. Some spoke with quiet assurance of their faith; some spoke of their religion as though they were trying by means of it to escape from anxiety and were not succeeding very well.

There was not enough material or enough of a common thread in the statements about religion to provide the basis for a separate chapter in this book. But one feature of the comments on religion does fit into the present context—the search for meaning.

Several people, when referring to religion, did so in what seemed to be a rather self-conscious manner, as though religion were hardly a proper thing to discuss when one teacher talks to another. In the opinion of the writer, this attitude is rather depressing, emphasizing again how people have been schooled to avoid sharing with others the things that concern them most. It is another symptom of a tendency to avoid the implications of the search for meaning.

Religion, if it means anything at all, has a profound and intimate personal meaning. The religious person, if he is sincere, seeks through his religion to find what to him is of ultimate concern. Religion is, at least for some, the utmost in the search for meaning. In the view of many people, the question of meaning a person raises when he asks, Who and what and why am I?, becomes a religious question when pursued to a final decision. For it raises other questions: What is the ground of my being? What is the foundation of my assurance that life is worth living? What is the substance on which I build my hope?

It is not just the credulous and unlearned or those seeking an easy escape who raise questions of religion. These questions face every scientist and every scholar when he has gone to the outermost reaches of his discipline, if not before. So it is anomalous that when questions of religion are raised in education, they are often raised apologetically—as though a person should apologize for seeking, or claiming to have found, the ultimate answer to the meaning of his life.

Humility

In this book humility has been mentioned as essential to the search for meaning. Why is this, and what is meant by humility?

Humility is a form of inner strength, a kind of dignity that makes it less necessary for a person to pretend.

It is something quite different from weakness. The humble one is not humble because he is spineless. To be humble is not the same as to be obsequious, or an easy mark, or a person without robust convictions.

Why is the one who seeks for meaning humble?

He cannot help but be humble when he looks beyond the appearances of things and contemplates the vast reaches of the unknown. The more he grows in understanding, the more he realizes how much there is that yet lies hidden. He realizes that he cannot see the distant scene, but he can accept this fact without bitterness.

He cannot help but be humble when he looks upon the marvel of human growth. What parent can contemplate, for example, the development of language in a child without a feeling of awe? What teacher has not had an experience of reverent wonder while watching the mental life of his pupils unfold?

When a person seeks to realize the meaning of his own emotions, he cannot help but be humble. He is baffled by the play of love and hate in his life. He cannot penetrate the clouds of anxiety that move across the horizons of his inner world. He is perplexed by the conditions that sometimes move him toward depths of longing. He is bewildered by the complexity of his feelings, which lead him at times to accept what he should reject and to reject what by rights he should accept. He is baffled by the worries that assail him and the forebodings that sometimes seize him.

He cannot help but be humble when he considers the poignancy of his grief; the weight of his melancholy on occasion; the inexpressible quality of the joy that sometimes wells up in him; the ominous waves that threaten to engulf him as he stands on the brink of despair; and the thrill that surges through him as he tastes in advance a happy fulfillment of his hopes.

He cannot help but feel humble as he absorbs all that he can know, and in so doing glimpses depths he can never fathom and heights he can never scale in the majestic peaks and valleys of his inner life.

What are the marks of one who is humble?

Above all, he is one who is able to wait and to be silent. He can wait, for he does not expect that he should immediately understand each question from within or have a response to each query from without. He can wait, for he does not expect to reach an instantaneous insight or to have an instantaneous answer or to offer an immediate competing or echoing remark when others speak. He does not feel guilty about not knowing—at least not always. Nor does he feel guilty when he is assailed by doubts concerning something he once thought he knew.

Being able to wait enables him to listen. He is a good listener when others have something to say, and he will hear them out if he thinks it is fit or timely to do so. But even more, he is a good listener to his own inner voice, which often speaks very slowly and indistinctly. If he were not a good listener, he would not give himself time to experience the impact of his feelings, to catch the meaning or at least to try to capture the meaning of a nascent mood or a vaguely pleasant or disquieting thought that crosses his mind.

This ability to wait and to listen is not just a cultivated pose. It is acquired only when a person has become able to dispense with some of his pretensions and has begun to learn not to make exorbitant demands upon himself. He is then able to appreciate, without enthusiasm but also without protest, the simple fact that so much in his life and in life about him is uncertain, untried, untested, and unknown.

There is a condition opposite to that of humility—a false

kind of pride and a harsh kind of arrogance, which cannot tolerate doubt. This arrogance is a form of anxiety. It is a condition of feeling mortally threatened unless one has immediately at hand the absolute and certain answers to questions pertaining to the nature of man's existence. When such an attitude prevails, a person cannot search for meaning; and even the meaning he has found, or thinks he has found, is probably only an academic possession. It is the kind of precarious truth embraced by one whose faith is so weak that he does not have courage to doubt.

The humble person can tolerate himself not only as one whose knowledge is imperfect but also as one who himself is imperfect. Here humility interweaves with compassion and provides a person with the beginning of wisdom. It is only when he can tolerate himself as an imperfect creature, without feeling apologetic about it, that he can have the freedom to listen and to learn.

The humble person is willing to accept truth and to seek it wherever it may be found. A humble teacher, for example, will accept a child as one who, in a given situation, may give a clearer and more profound glimpse into the meaning of things than the teacher himself. And a humble scholar is one who realizes that when a less learned person is puzzled and asks why, he may be more profound than the erudite person who knows the contents of a hundred books but never wonders what his erudition means.

FIVE

Sex

When teachers face themselves, one of the significant aspects of life they face is sex. An important characteristic of healthy selfhood is acceptance of one's sexual appetites and abilities.

Sex provides the consummate physical experience of self-fulfillment. It is also, for many, a stumbling block in the search for selfhood.

There is much about sex that is paradoxical. It is through sexual intimacy with a loved person that one realizes the deepest experience of relatedness to another human being. But it is also possible to enter into sexual experience with a kind of detachment that is the antithesis of relatedness to others. Sex may be an expression of tenderness, but it can also serve hate. It is a vehicle for sharing, but it can also be a means of giving without taking or taking without giving. It may be used as an instrument of conquest, as a means of venting hostility, as a tool for taking revenge, as an endeavor to assuage feelings of inferiority, as a relief from anxiety, as proof of one's manhood or womanhood, and so on.

One of the problems about sex is that it is often, in education and elsewhere, treated as a problem and as nothing else. Sex is an essential possession of one's being, a gift through which life has its most absorbing physical experience of life. One of the tragedies of our culture is that large numbers of human beings are unable to use or enjoy this gift. The lack of access to the sexual part of themselves may occur both among those who see sex as an aspect of a mechanistic life-process and among those who see it as a gift from the Creator.

Although there is perhaps hardly a parent or teacher in our culture who is not, or has not been, somewhat anxious about sex, the data obtained from those who participated in this study were limited.[1] Although sex was one of the categories represented on the Personal Issues Inventory, only about a third of the people identified it as an area in their lives in which they needed help in understanding themselves. The reasons for the comparative lack of mention of sex, both in interviews and on the Personal Issues Inventory, can be a matter of speculation only. Even in a therapeutic situation, of course, it often takes many sessions before some persons feel free to speak about sex. In the present study, interviews seldom numbered more than two or three. It is possible, also, that sex was not mentioned by many who did express concern over other difficulties because they felt that some of these difficulties were, in a sense, more fundamental.

The most self-revealing confidences concerning sexual problems would probably disclose that sex is not the sole problem, nor even the central problem. But regardless of this, many teachers undoubtedly have important problems relating to sex

[1] It is hoped to deal more fully with this topic in a later study.

that could be explored more thoroughly than it was possible to explore them here. This holds whether we believe (as some people still do) that sex is the key to all human perplexities or take the view (which is increasingly being advanced) that problems pertaining to sex are usually imbedded in a larger context of difficulty in relations with others and with oneself.

Many of those who raised sexual problems did so in the context of other concerns discussed in this book. One such concern was loneliness; both men and women spoke of being troubled because their sexual relations consisted, so it seemed to them, of a physical connection without any emotional closeness or psychological intimacy. Sexual problems were also discussed in the context of meaning and meaninglessness when people said, in effect, "I have sexual relations with this man (or woman), but he (or she) really doesn't mean anything to me; it is like going through some motions, and these motions alone don't matter enough." This concern about the meaning of sexual relations was expressed by some of the older persons among those interviewed. It is likely that it would be less prevalent among people in the full flush of youth, when sex is new, so to speak, and the biological urge to find a sexual "outlet" (as Kinsey so poetically puts it) is strong enough to sweep other considerations aside.

Some of the people who were interviewed complained about their sexual partners, as though they felt that they were being exploited. A few boasted about their sexual freedom, and yet the very fact that they boasted revealed that they were uneasy, as though recognizing that a person can move from one sexual adventure to another and still be a very lonely person, one who has not found anything meaningful in his relations with others or any substantial meaning within himself. Some spoke guiltily. Quite a few spoke with regret about sexual experiences they had not had, deploring the fact that they had avoided sex (and time was running short); others regretted sexual experiences they did not regard as measuring up to the promise of their own sexuality.

The people who participated in this study revealed many of the contrasting attitudes toward sex that can also be observed in everyday life, and it was impressive to note how these attitudes were tied to a larger pattern of attitudes toward others and themselves. Some people, for example, spoke of sex as something belonging to a larger emotional context, in which there is mutual regard and some tenderness and affection. At the other extreme, there were people who seemed to be sexual opportunists, whose only desire appeared to be to find physical release with someone who happened, at the moment, to strike their fancy.

The motives underlying these and other approaches to sex are, of course, diverse. The person who will accept the idea of sexual relations only with a person with whom he has already formed an emotional tie may be a person with a healthy set of values and a mature emotional outlook. On the other hand, he may be a frightened person who carries the idea of emotional affinity to such an extreme that he effectively cuts himself off from sex altogether. The motive of the sexual opportunist may be to make a conquest, or to establish a fleeting illusion of intimacy and closeness with another person, or to satisfy a gnawing need to prove his potency.

The fact that even a relationship involving two people as intimately as a sexual relationship may represent to one simply a passing desire to enjoy the sensations of the moment while, to the other, it represents a profoundly significant emotional experience is one circumstance, among many, that contributes to the problems of loneliness and meaninglessness, discussed elsewhere in this book.

In the sphere of sex, as in connection with other currents of life, there is a great deal of projection. Several people, in interviews, said in effect, "Sex has avoided me," when in reality they might better have said, "I have avoided sex." Some people find it less threatening to attribute their lack of courage to outer circumstances than to look into the role of evasion they themselves are playing. Projection of sexual problems also takes place when a person blames the unsatisfactoriness of sexual experiences he has had on others, without inquiring what his own responsibility in the matter might be.

In the writer's opinion, the relatively infrequent mention of sex by the participants in this study, even though the level of self-revelation was comparatively deep, is another indication of the great need in teacher-training to face the facts of life.

Every person feels the promptings of sex, which in their original form are healthy. By the time he is a teacher, and even long before, he may also have acquired impulses that are not so healthy, such as an anxious need to seek a solution for the problems of life through sex, as though it had a kind of magic, or a desperate desire to keep sex out of his life, as though it were a horrible threat. Yet in spite of the fact that sex is something of vital concern to all people, one can go to classes and take part in group discussions, committee meetings, curriculum conferences, symposia on needed research in education, and the like, and never hear any mention of sex, even when the discussions are supposed to deal with *real* concerns.

As long as we evade the issue of sex in education—in the

education of teachers and in the education of the children they teach—we are play-acting. This does not mean that we have to magnify sex as the only real problem in life, for it is not. Neither should we minimize it as something subsidiary, for it is not something subsidiary. As long as we remain aloof from this aspect of life (wholly or by relegating it to a little unit on sex education), we are promoting and abetting the conditions contributing to other problems so many of the teachers who took part in this study found disturbing—loneliness, meaninglessness, anxiety, obsequious or rebellious attitudes toward authority, homelessness, and hopelessness.

Call it what we will, sex, Eros, the emotion tied to life's passion to renew life, cannot be denied. Whether we regard it as an expression of human love or as an elemental physical force, we must face its power and seek to be at home with its promptings if we would take the first step toward accepting or understanding ourselves.

SIX

Hostility

To face anger and hostility as an aspect of one's life, one must draw to the fullest extent upon one's capacity for self-acceptance, sympathy, and understanding. Anger and hostility affect us all. They are inevitable.

Anger is linked from an early age to a person's efforts to protect himself from interference by others. It is mobilized when a person's wishes are thwarted, and is linked as a primitive emotional companion to the child's earliest strivings. In a sense, we may call anger the handmaiden of a child's earliest efforts to assert himself and to be himself. As long as life lasts, anger, although it is often misplaced and takes foolish turns, is an essential factor in a human being's effort to be a person in his own right.

With the passage of time, children not only show anger that flares on the occasion and then subsides; they also acquire attitudes of hostility, a lingering or residual form of potential anger that persists beyond the occasion. Attitudes of hostility, as is noted in more detail later, may prevail in the form of grievances or a chronic disposition to have a chip on one's shoulder. They may appear in a tendency to be sarcastic. They may prevail in the form of prejudices, or in a tendency to bristle or rebel (or to cringe) when dealing with an authority figure, or in a tendency to become angered by little annoyances that, objectively, do not merit so much wrath. Attitudes of hostility may also appear in a tendency to be defensive or suspicious or to assume that others have unfriendly intentions, or in a compulsion to strike the first blow (especially by way of a cutting or belittling remark). Hostility may appear in the form of activities and interests that, on the surface, have the mark of pure scholarship.

While hostility is usually unpleasant, it is also inevitable. It is impossible to face all the demands of life without feeling put upon. It is impossible to meet the many unavoidable frustrations of life without becoming angry. And repeated experiences of anger may lead to an attitude of hostility. It is probably impossible for even the best students, under the best conditions, to submit to rules and regulations and all the requirements that come under the heading of discipline without feeling at times that others are thwarting, blocking, or coercing them. Even under the best circumstances, in the hands of the most skillful parent and the most competent teacher, discipline is likely, at times, to have a bitter taste. Life is such that rules must be imposed. It is in the nature of discipline that it is something first imposed from without, not spontaneously from within. Somewhere along the way, a person is bound to feel aggrieved.

Hostility, while it originally grows out of a person's efforts to protect and preserve his individuality, eventually entails a vast amount of suffering. There is suffering when a person carries a burden of hostility like a leftover load from an earlier day. This burden weighs heavily on the people against whom the hostility is directed, but it often weighs more heavily on the one who is hostile.

Hostility is painful to the person who harbors it. Frequently, in childhood, it (or the earlier, simpler expression of anger) is punished by the person against whom it is directed. Much happens to drive hostility underground. It is often very elusive, so elusive that people frequently do not even suspect how much they are governed by it. Hostility appears in many disguises, which fool others and also fool the hostile person himself. It often works like Satan in the garb of a saint. People who undergo therapy or psychoanalysis often find that their hostile tendencies are hard to grasp even after they have made considerable progress in understanding themselves.

Recognition of hostile tendencies is of great value to a person seeking to understand himself. Hostile attitudes (if one can catch a glimpse of them) and angry moods (if one has the courage to consider what they mean) can give significant clues to self-discovery. Moreover, hostility in an older person, like anger in a young child, often serves as the means (although often rather awkward and misdirected) by which a person preserves his right to be himself or realizes his right to assert himself. Sometimes it is by way of hostility that a compulsively compliant person first begins to show that he is waking up, so to speak. His hostility may at first be misplaced—he feels hostile toward people who have pushed him around and taken advantage of him, perhaps not realizing at first that it is he who has invited them to do so. But a wave of anger such as this may be the beginning of a healthy process of self-repair if, in due time, the person begins to perceive that the abuse inflicted upon him by others he has in reality brought on himself.

In the present study all the people who were interviewed expressed hostility, some openly, some by indirection. Many probably would have denied vehemently any suggestion by the interviewer that they were expressing hostility—for example, by heatedly describing the faults or frailties of others. ("The other teachers in my school are frightfully unbalanced, and the cultural level of teachers is horribly low.") Hostility was also expressed through self-criticism. Several people spoke of their difficulty in meeting the high expectations they placed on themselves. One, for example, mentioned inability to be lenient with respect to her own inadequacies. Another spoke of the exorbitant demand placed on himself by the feeling that he should know all the answers.

Many of the people interviewed showed their hostility through grievances. Some complained about administrators, colleagues, and students. They griped about restrictions; working conditions; salaries; the rigidity of the administrative hierarchy; the superior attitudes assumed by people in superior positions; the demands placed upon them by parents, children, or other teachers; and so on. Such complaints often have a realistic basis. But there is evidence of disguised hostility when a person looks upon everyone and everything else as being in the wrong.

The four statements that, in the preparation of the Personal Issues Inventory, were selected as representing more or less consciously recognized hostility were the following: "I sometimes lose my temper or have feelings of anger or intense rage that disturb me; I often feel bitter and resentful at being pushed around or imposed on by others without being free to complain or show my resentment; Even though I try to get along smoothly with others, so often other people don't really consider my feelings; I have a feeling that one must be on guard and not take things lying down, for people will take advantage of you." Of those who responded to the Inventory, about half identified one or more of the statements as descriptive of an area in which they probably needed help in understanding themselves.

The four statements listed above give only a meager clue to the role of hostility in the lives of teachers. Hostility often appears in actions and states of mind that do not contain any clear element of anger and that seem utterly devoid of any motive to inflict hurt or to take revenge.

Externalized Hostility

One of the commonest ways of dealing with hostility is to externalize it—to state the "problem" in terms of what is wrong with others, or to attribute to others a state of being angry or bitter or unfair. The fact that anger is usually a rather painful emotion, coupled with the fact that all children, from an early age, are under pressure not to show or even feel it, makes it necessary for us to avoid the sharp impact of our own anger by pretending that it is not we who are angry but someone else who is angry or in the wrong.

As already noted, many of those interviewed in connection with this study spoke of their problems as though they existed outside themselves and could be blamed entirely on some situation or person. One individual, for example, who revealed many personal problems, spent most of his time talking about how "frightfully in need" of help other people were. Many of the teachers discussed their problems as existing exclusively in the behavior and attitudes of their pupils. Actually, many of their pupils were very irritating; but the problem of hostility cannot be faced by simply listing the faults of others.

110

The Feeling of Being Abused

In one of her most revealing writings, Horney (15) has discussed the feeling of being abused in a manner that is helpful both for understanding oneself and for understanding others. She points out that the feeling of being abused may at first be based on a hard core of reality, but that it becomes especially troublesome when irrational elements are added to it. Every child in a sense *is* an abused person. Even if his parents and teachers are perfect models of patience and reasonableness—which no parent or teacher could possibly be—he is bound here or there to meet people in authority, or among his peers, or in the neighborhood at large, who vent their hostilities upon him. Further, he must yield to rules and restrictions, necessary for society, which he would not impose upon himself and which often seem foolish, coercive, and unfair.

But the feeling of being abused can readily go beyond the sphere of righteous and realistic anger to an attitude that is unrealistic. A child, for example, may feel abused, with some justification, because of what his teacher demands, and be angry. Now let us say that after having been angered he becomes guarded, defensive, and inclined to be rebellious. This attitude is likely to arouse anger or annoyance in the teacher, who is then short with him or otherwise punishes him. Now a vicious circle may be started. The child gets a chip on his shoulder. He may be overly ready to take offense. He may see others through the haze of his feeling of having been mistreated, and so even when people come to him with good intentions, he may see them as coming with bad intentions.

111

As has already been suggested, there are many circumstances in life at school that aggravate feelings of being abused —circumstances such as examinations, excessive homework, strict rules and regulations. Each of these may be justifiable as far as the teacher is concerned, but if a student is already inclined to put his own sour interpretation on things, his feeling of being abused will be intensified. This feeling may be embroidered and elaborated until the person is out of touch with the original and realistic basis for feeling aggrieved.

One of the devices of the adult who feels abused is to review his childhood and, through an elaborate afterthought, to build up a rationale of himself as having been an abused child. There may be strong elements of truth in this rationale. Perhaps his parents were unduly severe. Maybe he was rejected. Maybe he was the victim of cruel people in his school or in his neighborhood. But the afterthought may also contain much that is irrational. A person may use selective recall, so that in looking back on his life, he seizes only upon events that fit his present need to find someone or something to blame. When this happens, he is projecting his present hostility upon conditions in his own earlier life. Accordingly, when a person, in his own thoughts or in his conversation with others, dwells in an aggrieved way on how tough a time he had as a child, he may or may not be giving a realistic account of his childhood, but he is definitely revealing hostile attitudes prevailing in the present.

Another quite common form of projecting feelings of being abused is to think in a mood of resentment or self-pity of the social class one was reared in, or to blame all the woes of life on economic circumstances. There is no denying that economic circumstances do have an important bearing on a person's life, but they may also be used as a substitute target and as a scapegoat for feelings of resentment that might better be faced openly and directly in an effort to deal with one's hostility in a rational way.

Using the Arts of Love
to Accomplish the Purposes of Hate

Many conditions of hostility are so subtle and so thoroughly disguised that they are difficult to detect.

Sometimes hostility is disguised as love. There are people, for example, whose hostility takes the form of an insatiable need for power over others, and who dominate others with seeming kindness. They may be extremely "nice," "thoughtful," and "considerate" in the eyes of those they are trying to bend to their will. The arts of love may be used as instruments of hate.

The arts of love are sometimes used in a hostile way by parents and teachers who are overprotective in their dealings with children. One way to reject a child is to go through the motions of doing everything for him and giving him everything he wants except the one thing he most needs—to be warmly accepted for his own sake.

Seductiveness is another way of using the arts of love in the service of hostility. This kind of seductiveness may be practiced without having any obvious sexual connotations, although at adolescence and beyond the seducer often uses sexual motivation as a means of conquest. A teacher may employ a wide range of lures to get students to "fall" for him. He may compete with parents for students' affection, or try to make them loyal to himself and to no one else. He may use every known device to appear more understanding, attractive, lovable, entrancing, and wonderful than any other teacher in the school. He may flatter, notice little things that mean a lot, perform thoughtful acts, and in many ways prey upon the victims' hunger for attention and approval and love. But the aim of such a seducer is not to go out to others with whole-hearted love and friendliness. His hidden aim is to make others abjectly attached to him and then, later, to reject them.[1]

One of the driving forces in a hostile person who uses the arts of love to hurt others may be an unrecognized need to take revenge. Old hurts may have left so sharp a sting that he must get even, although he does not recognize this to be the case. Old wounds may have left pains so deep that someone has to pay. Old injuries to the pride may have been so harsh that someone else must suffer. When such a drive prevails, there is hostility in one of its most pitiable forms. Such a hostile person is a sick person. He is so sick that he will use even the sweetest syllables in the language of love and the tenderest gestures in the art of loving to accomplish his bitter end.

There are always people waiting to become victims of seduction. All human beings have a great hunger for approval and affection, and in some people, and at certain points in the lives of all people, this hunger may be so overpowering that a semblance of affection is accepted as though it were the real thing.

There are people so starved for attention that whatever someone else offers, no matter what his underlying motive may be, is like a precious gift.

[1] A powerful account of the demonic craftiness of this kind of motivation has been given in Kierkegaard's classic "Diary of the Seducer," a section of *Either/Or* (33).

Hostility in Education

In an earlier chapter it was stated that hostility is prevalent in education. While there are innumerable teachers who are as genuine and as generous in their attitudes toward students as it is possible for a human being to be, there are also many others who are punitive or who unthinkingly carry out punitive practices.

One of the most obvious manifestations of hostility in education appears in the feuds that sometimes prevail between members of the teaching staff. When a person is involved in a long-continued, bitter feud, it is likely that unresolved hostile tendencies carried over from his earlier experience, rather than the unpleasantness or unfairness of the people with whom he is carrying on the feud, are responsible for his difficulties. There are many expressions of hostility, however, that are less obvious than an open feud.

As was mentioned earlier, we are venting hostility or serving as the instruments of hostile attitudes when we needlessly expose students to failure and humiliating criticism. One general expression of hostility in the academic world is to treat difficulty in learning as a deliberate kind of rebellion, which should be punished. There is also an undercurrent of hostility in intellectual snobbery. We are venting hostility when we feel contempt for people who are not as bright as ourselves or who, as we see it, have academic wares that are inferior to our own.

There are many practices in education that, in the writer's opinion, directly or indirectly express hostility even though the element of hostility may seem rather remote. For example, it is hard to account for the rigidities that appear in course requirements and in courses of study, or for the great areas of meaninglessness discussed earlier in this book, particularly at the high school and college levels, without assuming that somebody had a great need for pushing somebody else around. These rigidities may, of course, become so commonplace and hallowed by tradition that it is not easy to trace the hostility to those who are most responsible.

A teacher may act as an agent or instrument of hostility even though he is not noticeably hostile while performing the act. He may show passive acquiescence in policies that express hostility. This happens, in the writer's opinion, when school people slavishly and without a second thought impose arbitrary academic requirements that happen to be unsuited to many students just because someone, somewhere, at some time, had the power to write his own prejudices into the curriculum.

Again, it is perhaps only by assuming hostility or acquiescence in hostility that we can account for so much that goes by default in school systems. For example, in many schools with elaborate budgets for other things, the provisions for guidance or therapy for seriously disturbed pupils are woefully inadequate and the methods of dealing with such pupils very cruel. Many teachers, of course, struggle as best they can against such cruelty; obviously they cannot be accused of being hostile just because they are staff members in a school where children are ill-treated. But we certainly can suspect hostility when administrators and teachers are complacent about such mistreatment or even abet it.

Even scholarliness may function as an expression of hostility. This can be seen most obviously when scholarly disputes are expressions of personal animosities between scholars. The violence and sarcasm that creep into scientific papers are also an illustration. Book reviewing often provides an outlet for hostile feelings. When hostility crops out in these ways, we are probably right in assuming that it is usually interwoven with a mixture of other motives. The person who is hostile may also be moved by a strong desire to further what he regards as the truth.

During the course of a week spent in observing one's own attitudes and the open and disguised feelings of others in the teaching profession, it would be possible to get a great pile of data on the play of hostility in the professional activities of the scholar and the teacher. And why not? Scholars and teachers are human, too. We would probably get as large a pile, or an even larger one, if we observed people in some of the other professions.

To say that hostility enters so freely into the life of the scholar and the teacher is not to find fault. It does provide another point of emphasis, however, for the theme of this book, namely, that we, as teachers, need to face ourselves. The blinder our hostility is, the harsher we are likely to be with others and with ourselves. The more courage and humility we can bring to bear in facing our hostility, the less destructive it is likely to be.

Attitudes toward Authority

It is usually in relations with parents and parent substitutes that the conditions leading to hostility first occur. As children grow older, attitudes toward parents and toward other authority figures in their early years color their attitudes toward other people. This process continues even when, supposedly, they have become independent and responsible people in their own right.

Judging from what one can observe in everyday life, there

is a vast amount of carry-over of childhood attitudes toward authority into adulthood. One sees it in the sudden change in atmosphere in a group when the boss or the chief or someone with seniority or greater prestige enters. People who have been informal stiffen into a posture of respect. The free and easy exchange of small talk ceases. The one who was telling a ribald story suddenly becomes prim. Those who previously were bored now hang on the words of Mr. or Mrs. Big, even when their pronouncements are quite inane.

One of the many fascinating observations in group therapy is that old attitudes of resentment toward the father or mother can be triggered off by people who for one reason or another symbolize these characters, even though objectively they are quite different. Thus, to one participant, a woman with certain "strong" traits may represent the strong father; and a man, to another man or woman, may represent a demanding mother. An older person's attitudes toward authority may be projected onto a younger person, and so on.

Many of the people interviewed in this study voiced problems concerning their attitudes toward, or their relations with, people in authority, and the category of attitudes toward authority was included in the Personal Issues Inventory. Although not all those who indicated that they needed help with this aspect of their relations with others were thereby expressing hostility, many obviously did voice some kind of resentment. One of the four statements pertaining to authority expresses rebellion. Another expresses annoyance at being put upon because of a tendency to yield too readily to demands from others. (In connection with this, it may be noted that parents and teachers sometimes invest children with authority and allow themselves to be pushed around to an unreasonable extent.) One statement, without openly expressing resentment, reveals a tendency to be put upon or subdued when in the presence of a person who is seen as a superior; it is likely that where such a curtailment of freedom occurs, there is often an undercurrent of resentment. The fourth statement describes a strong tendency to conform—to act according to the standards of others rather than personal convictions. Often, no doubt, a person who expresses this kind of coercion (which may be largely self-imposed) feels resentment, but this can only be inferred.

Of the group of 229 people who responded to the Personal Issues Inventory, fifty-five per cent recorded that relations with people in authority represented an area in which they probably needed help in understanding themselves.

Attitudes toward authority constitute one of the most important problems teachers must face when they face themselves. Here, as is true of all the topics discussed in this book, the problem is primarily a subjective one. It cannot be resolved simply by manipulating external circumstances. Many naive forms of such manipulation have been widely used in educational circles to deal with "status" problems— that is, problems pertaining to attitudes toward authority figures. Everyone is called only by his first name. Professional titles are dropped, so that there are no doctors or professors. The administrator becomes very folksy and informal. People sit in a circle so that there is no head of the table. A teacher delegates management to a class committee. Lectures are abandoned and only the discussion method is used. And so on, ad infinitum.

These devices may, in some circumstances, produce a cozy sort of atmosphere. But to deal only with externals may leave the basic attitudes completely untouched. Much that is illusory takes place in the name of "democratic procedures," although these procedures are probably good as far as they go. But even in a situation that has every appearance of being democratic, there is a great amount of projection of personal attitudes. To get at these, something more is needed than the presence of a benign authority figure who goes through the motions of sharing his authority. Actually, the official authority figure may not, for all members of the group, be the psychological authority figure. What is essential is a climate in which people are free to express their feelings regarding one another and to uncover feelings they themselves do not recognize but others may.

Hostility, Guilt, and Anxiety

Hostility, guilt, and anxiety are closely linked. We touched on this when we discussed theories concerning the role of hostility in anxiety. Hostile attitudes, whether or not clearly perceived for what they are, are frightening. They are frightening to a child because his hostility is usually directed against those upon whom he most depends, and who therefore have the greatest power of retaliation. The people who give offense are likely also to be those the child goes to for love and protection. It is dangerous to strike out against them. It is threatening even to have the impulse to do so, for this impulse involves inner conflict. There is conflict between the impulse to love and the impulse to hate, between the surge of the child's anger and his impulse to be a grateful offspring.

These childhood conflicts related to hostility are likely to persist into later years. By the time we are old enough to be teachers—or even to enter training for teaching—most of us have been schooled for years in suppressing and repressing our hostility. But the residue of grievances and resentments may still be there. Although we may be blind to it, we are stuck with it, and blindly driven by it, unless or until we can face some of its meanings.

Many of the conditions that caused resentment in childhood may also persist into later years. This happens when a teacher in his twenties—and even in his forties and fifties—is still dominated in obvious or subtle ways by his father or mother. The dominating parent may to all appearances be a kindly and benign person, but a parent who seems kind can be as coercive as one who seems unkind. Parental domination can continue even if this older teacher's parents are dead or live far away and seldom cross his path. Such a teacher, although he is old, may be in conflict (much as a child might be) if, on the one hand, he is coerced and dominated by the image and memory and teachings of his parents, and, on the other, he rebels against this domination and resentfully resists this coercion but is unable to recognize what is happening and cannot allow himself even to *feel* his anger, let alone face it and strive to deal with it in a rational way.

One who has angry thoughts and vengeful feelings that go against what he regards as his better nature feels guilty. A teacher cannot help recoiling when he has a "death wish," as he does when he secretly, for an instant, has a feeling of relief on hearing that a principal he dislikes has been in an accident and his mind leaps to the thought that it might be fatal, but in a flash he dismisses the thought. There is a murderous thought, too, when he hears that his most troublesome pupil is sick, and his racing fancies see this pupil out of the way forever—and then in the same instant the fancy fades. This wish that another person be dead or forever out of the way may be so fleeting that the teacher does not recognize it for what it is. Yet although fleeting and not fully recognized, it is an outcropping of hostility of a kind he has been trained from childhood to suppress, and therefore it is disquieting and likely to produce guilt and anxiety. The guilt and anxiety that flow from such murderous impulses are likely to be especially acute unless this teacher can learn, to some degree, to accept hostility as an aspect of his existence and to be at home with himself as a hostile person. When he can do this, he will accept himself as one who has hostile impulses, without feeling a brutal compulsion to punish himself—or others—for them. He may even be able to smile indulgently when someone quips that a death wish a day keeps the doctor away.

For one who has long suppressed his hostility, denying himself the right to be angry at those who thwart him, it is very difficult to regain the ability to feel a full-bodied surge of anger or an upwelling of rage. The old sequence of events in childhood through which suppression took place—anger, the impulse to attack, fear of attacking and of retaliation (or guilt because the impulse to attack conflicts with the impulse to love and to seek love), and anxiety tied to these conflicting impulses—can have so powerful an effect that it is almost impossible for an older person to acquire again the ability to be angry in a forthright and spontaneous way. This does not mean that such people are never angry. They may actually be irascible people who are hard to get along with, but their anger is devious and rooted in conflict. A person who does not have the freedom to be angry, and to direct his anger against the real offender, may turn the anger against himself, as happens when a person suffering from guilt (which is a kind of self-imposed punishment) abuses his health or places himself in a situation where he will meet a painful accident. Or he may blindly take out his anger on others, as happens when a teacher does not face the conditions that have actually angered him but is hostile toward his students or quarrels with colleagues who happen to be convenient targets but had nothing to do with the origins of his hostility.

The Right to Be Angry

There are many people who have, to a large extent, surrendered the right to be angry. These people are not limited to those who keep turning the other cheek when even the one who seriously advocates this policy would begin to use a flail. Among those who have surrendered the right to anger there are some, as noted above, who actually show a great deal of anger. There is a difference between freedom to be sarcastic or to hit someone in the teeth and freedom to accept within oneself the full force, meaning, and impact of this simple condition: I am an angry person.

Some people actually strike out at others (with fists or polite phrases) in a desperate effort to ward off and block the full sweep of an upsurge of anger within themselves. One way to blunt awareness of one's own anger is to make it seem that the other person is really the hostile one and the one who started the fight. If the other person shows antagonism, there is, in a sense, justification for one's own anger. Shifting responsibility in this way means, in effect, throwing one's anger out, making it a social phenomenon rather than a personal possession, before one has fully taken it home to oneself.

When a person is able fully and freely to accept the fact that he is angry, he is less likely to hit out than he would be if he tried rather desperately, in mid-phase, so to speak, to "do something" about his anger. To accept oneself as a person who is subject to anger and who often does become angry means that one can allow oneself to become aware of what the anger is about and thereby deal with the anger-producing circumstance more effectively.

To accept oneself as an angry person also means to accept oneself as a person who has the right to draw on his capacity for anger. This is important, for there are many situations in which anger is appropriate and even necessary.

In its full expression, acceptance of oneself as a human being who has a capacity and a susceptibility for rage means that one is able to accept oneself even if one is *foolishly* angry (who isn't, at times?), or *unjustifiably* angry (what human being is there who has not often been angry without justification, as seen by others or by his own afterthoughts?), or even *maliciously* angry (who conforms so perfectly to an exalted, idealized image of himself that he does not allow himself once in a while—perhaps only by way of a fleeting thought—to feel malice toward someone else?).

Observe that this concept of accepting oneself as a human being who, like all humans, is given to anger is something radically different from giving way to anger in a blind way, by punishing others or brutally punishing oneself. It is different from a self-righteous condoning of one's anger. To accept oneself as an angry person, as one who is *subject* to anger, as one who has the *right* to be angry, as one who can *forgive himself* even for being stupidly angry, is to succeed in one of the most difficult aspects of the struggle for self-acceptance. If one has succeeded in this struggle, or partially so, it does not mean that one will henceforth be above anger, or always deal with it in a beautifully "integrated" way. But one thing can be counted on. A person who has made some progress in this aspect of the struggle for self-acceptance is likely to feel his anger in a more healthy way, to deal with it more constructively, and to live with it in a fashion that will bring far less needless suffering to himself and to others.

SEVEN

Compassion

Wwhen teachers face themselves, they face a hard struggle; but they may also look forward to great rewards. The greatest of these rewards is growth in compassion.

Compassion is inextricably linked to acceptance of self and of others. It is the ultimate expression of emotional maturity. It is through compassion that a person experiences the highest peak and the deepest reach in his search for self-understanding.

We often think of compassion as something soft, perhaps touched with sentimentality. Compassion sometimes has this connotation, but it also has a more profound psychological meaning. There is something soft and tender in compassion, but also something rugged and very hard. To be compassionate, one must be able to accept the impact of any emotion—love or hate, joy, fear, or grief—tolerate it and harbor it long enough and with sufficient absorption to accept its meaning and to enter into a fellowship of feeling with the one who is moved by the emotion. This is the heroic feature of compassion in its fullest development: to be able to face the ravage

of rage, the shattering impact of terror, the tenderest promptings of love, and then to embrace these in a larger context,
which involves an acceptance of these feelings and an appre-
ciation of what they mean to the one who experiences them.

To be compassionate means to partake in passion: the
passions of others, the passions that arise within oneself. It
means to participate in feeling rather than simply to view it
as a spectator might. It is a way of entering into emotional
fellowship. It means to take feeling home to oneself as one
who is willing and has the strength to sustain its power and
realize its force. Compassion is stronger than anger, mightier
than love, more powerful than fear. It gives the measure of
a person's strength as a human being. It is not the emotion of
the weak. It is the hard-gotten property of the strong.

The compassionate person is not just one who goes out in
a good-hearted manner to someone who is having a tough
time. He loves, but he also hates. He partakes in courage,
but also in fear. He partakes in joy, but also in grief. The
compassionate person is not just one who goes about with
sweet emotions, for he also enters into life's harshness and
bitterness. The range of compassion is the range of human
emotion.

Anger may be used to provide one illustration of compassion. To be compassionate with one who is enraged means that
one allows oneself to enter into the meaning of this rage. It
does not mean that, at the moment of compassion, one becomes
as enraged as the other person. If one did, one would be so
absorbed in rage as the primary emotion that there would be
no room for compassion. Neither does it mean that one feels
sorry for the one who is angry (one might feel sorry, but that
is not the essence of compassion), nor that one deplores his
anger (one might feel that the anger is deplorable, but that is

126

not compassion). The primary quality of compassion as it pertains to anger is to feel the impact and to savor the meaning of the emotion of anger. This does not mean that one condones it, nor that one hastens to confirm the angry person in his anger, nor that one joins the fray to fight with the person against whom the anger is directed. One might or might not, as a separate consideration, do any of these things. To be compassionate with one who is angry is to know, in an emotional way, the nature of anger.

To feel compassion for one who is angry means that one must draw upon one's own capacity for anger and one's experience of anger. One realizes, as it were, through a process of fellow-feeling, the rack and grind of anger, the bitterness of it, the driven character of it, the helpless way in which one can be possessed by it, the impulse to rend and destroy that goes with it, the self-hate that is often involved in it, the suffering and guilt that sometimes ensue from it. To feel compassion for one who is angry means to enter into the meaning of what it might be if one were that angry oneself. It means, for the moment, a kind of *acceptance* of the fact and the state of anger.

To feel compassion for one who is joyful or sad, one must draw upon one's capacity for joy or sorrow in order to realize what these emotions consist of and what their quality might be, as a personal experience, to those who rejoice or sorrow. To feel compassion for one who is frightened or lonely or sexually aroused, or hungry or jealous or anxious, or in a mood of tenderness or melancholy, one must be able to draw upon one's own resources for experiencing what these appetites, moods, and emotions mean.

Why is compassion so intimately tied to understanding and acceptance of self and others? The answers have already been implied. First, to understand another person we must be able to realize not simply what he is thinking but also what he is feeling. It is not enough to know what is in his mind; it is essential also to know what is in his heart. Second, to understand oneself one must be able to be at home with one's own emotions. This second condition is essential to the first.

If I would understand another's anger, I must be able to face my own anger, taste it, be at home with it, *know* it in the deepest emotional connotation of that word. I cannot know my anger if anger in me is immediately clouded over and obscured with a feeling of guilt; if, *before I permit myself to feel it*, I have already passed judgment on it. To know my anger *I must accept myself, for the time being, as an angry person*, as one who has the right to be angry, as one whose right to anger should be respected. I may have many second thoughts about this or that episode of anger, perhaps feel sorry about it, or foolish, or realize that I was too quick to take offense. As an afterthought, when I have been just a little angry, I might even feel that had I been equal to the occasion, I would have gone into a towering rage, for one who accepts himself is able to become passionately angry. And so on. These considerations are important, but only of secondary importance. The essence of compassion is to enter into the emotion itself.

When one thus enters into, and in this sense seeks to accept, to know, to feel the impact of one's own emotions, one is compassionate toward oneself. This is essential to compassion for others. I cannot, for example, accept another's fear in a compassionate way unless I can accept myself as a person who is frightened now and then, or who once was a very frightened child.

Let us look briefly at compassion in relation to another

emotion—the emotion of joy, although usually we do not think of compassion as pertaining to gladness. One can be compassionate in relation to joy only to the extent that one is able to draw upon one's own capacity for it, one's ability to savor it, relish it, be at home with it as one who deserves to be joyful and has the right to rejoice. One cannot share joy unless one possesses it oneself. If one had the money or the power one might, of course, do much to provide means or situations from which others obtain joy. But this is not the same as compassion. The ability to be compassionate with one who is joyful—whether this one be another or oneself—implies the highest degree of self-acceptance and should perhaps be regarded as the farthest reach of self-fulfillment.

To be compassionate means, among other things, that we view emotion from the standpoint of self-fulfillment. When we look at emotion in this way, we have a kind of accounting quite different from what we usually think of.

Ordinarily we might say that to love fully, one should cast out hate. But to love is not to surrender the ability to hate, for the one who loves deeply often hates intensely. The condition that rules out love, if there is such a condition, is fear: fear that keeps one from loving or hating or rejoicing or drawing upon any and all of the emotions that flourish when one is oneself.

One might say that if one had enough courage, one would be without fear. But courage does not mean the absence of fear: the one who has courage to be himself will dare to face frightening things. Similarly, to be joyful does not mean that one must exclude sorrow, for the one who can rejoice most fully is the one who most exposes himself to sorrow. The one who takes a chance at joyful self-fulfillment takes the risk of shattering disappointment. But if sorrow takes the place of joy, the one who has the courage to be himself would rather feel sorrow than feel nothing. The condition that is farthest removed from feeling joyful or sorrowful is to feel nothing.

The opposite of despair is not simply a condition of hope or even a state of faith. Rather, the opposite of despair, if there is an opposite, is self-acceptance and compassion.

Love of Self and Love for Others

The concept of compassion incorporates the meaning of love for others and for oneself. Compassion involves self-acceptance and acceptance of others in the profoundest sense. The person who can most fully accept himself is the one who can most fully accept others. The one who accepts himself seeks to know the meaning and to grasp the impact of what is happening in his own inner life, and he is responsive to what is happening to others. The relation between acceptance of self and acceptance of others is emphasized in many current writings, and apparently it needs to be re-emphasized. In talks with other teachers, the writer has again and again met with objections to the concepts of self-acceptance and self-understanding on grounds that amount to self-rejection and a denial of compassion.

Some people object to the idea of self-acceptance on the ground that a person who accepts himself is smug and in danger of becoming falsely complacent. Actually, the self-accepting person is anything but smug. Another objection, touching on the concept of anxiety in relation to self-acceptance, is that instead of helping people to become less anxious, we should make them more anxious; only if people are anxious will they have an incentive to learn. Both of these views are based on a concept of motivation that reflects a punitive attitude toward self and others.

Still another objection is that the concepts of self-acceptance and self-understanding involve a futile kind of introspection. According to this view, in order really to get things done we should direct our thoughts outward and not inward. But just doing something is not in itself valuable or meaningful. In seeking to know oneself, one tries to understand the motives that are involved when one sets out to get things done. Without such self-examination, what one sees may be distorted and what one does may be without much meaning.

It has also been said that what we need in education is more self-denial rather than more self-acceptance. In the writer's judgment, an objection such as this represents a form of self-rejection and rejection of others, coupled with misunderstanding of the underlying idea.

The notion that it is only by self-denial that one can be of service to others deserves special attention. The idea that love of others and love of self are incompatible is widely held. Actually, this idea goes counter to fact; and it also collides with some widely held rules of conduct, such as the admonition to love one's neighbor as oneself. This admonition embodies both love of self and love for others; it definitely does not imply that one should hate oneself in order to love others. As Fromm, Horney, and Sullivan have emphasized, hatred of self is linked to hatred of others; without healthy love of self there can be no genuine love for anyone else.

Many of the teachers who were interviewed in this study expressed or implied the belief that it is only by denying oneself that one can serve others. Some seemed to think that the really devoted teacher gives much and takes nothing.

131

There are, of course, many people in the teaching profession who seem to live according to this belief. There are teachers who go all out in helping others without demanding any rights for themselves. There are some who tolerate acute discomfort without feeling that they have a right to see to their own comfort. There are some who believe they must suffer fools gladly without having the right to be foolish themselves. There are some who seem to think that they should be able to absorb the bitter anger of others without having the right to be angry themselves. There are some who think that they should go out in love to all creatures but that it is not proper for them to ask for love, or to seek it, or to demand it with a kind of savage passion.

A teacher who tries to go out to others but who cannot come home to himself and experience emotion *in his own right* may be noble, but he is not actually realizing his potentialities as a teacher. He stops at the halfway mark. Sacrifice of self is not compassion. One can devote oneself to others in a compulsive way, as a means of escaping anxiety or atoning for guilt. In order to make one's efforts in behalf of others really count, one must do more than go through the motions of being a good-hearted person. One must be an understanding person. One must be an accepting and compassionate person.

One cannot understand another's hurts in a manner that will enable one to minister to him most effectively unless one has enough concern for oneself to realize and to appreciate what it means in one's own experience to be hurt. One cannot understand another's hunger for affection, nor sense his craving for being accepted, nor realize how starved he is for companionship, unless one can draw upon one's own realization of what this hunger means and what the nature of the experience is by which the hungry one can be filled.

Without self-acceptance a teacher may, to be sure, accomplish much for others and teach them many things. The good he does may even exceed his own capacity, for the one who is desperately seeking a friend may read into the teacher's friendly acts an emotional content they do not actually possess. But to go all out, to *feel for* others (as distinguished from going through the motions of *doing* for others), to *feel with* others (as distinguished from going through the motions of *cooperating* with them), it is essential that the teacher draw upon his own capacity for feeling. And he can do this only if he respects his feelings and is at home with them, if he accepts them as part of himself. This means self-acceptance, which involves compassion for oneself.

Where there is a lack of ability to accept oneself and one's own feelings, the process of giving, as has been suggested above, may be an unhealthy compulsion. One person may be as greedy to give as another is to take, and for motives that are much the same. For the moment, compulsive giving may be very satisfying to the one who receives, but in the long run it is not. One can see this at times when one observes the reaction of children to adults. Here is an adult who comes laden with gifts. He plays the games the children want to play. He defers to every whim and wish, and his patience and forbearance seem inexhaustible. But after a time the children tire of him. He is boring. They look on him as something of a stuffed shirt. Here comes another; his bosom does not swell only with bounty for others. He joins the children in play, but he also has some ideas of his own about how and what to play. His patience is thin at times, he gets annoyed, and in other ways now and then his emotions show through. But somehow he has a spark; the kids get sore at him, but they want him to come back. And when one of them is in trouble, he goes to this person rather than to the one who is so generous in such a deadly way. One brings his bounty; the other brings himself.

So Small in the Infinite
Scheme of Things—

In education there are many influences that emphasize the importance of quantity, number, and size. Many teachers assume, almost as though it were in the nature of things, that to learn a lot about a subject is better than to learn a little. We often take for granted in our measurements that large numbers are better than small numbers. We have to look far to find one who would not take it for granted that a high I Q is better than a low I Q. And so on.

When we enter the sphere of selfhood, however, these quantities, numbers, and dimensions are not so important. When we deal with the concepts of selfhood, self-acceptance, and self-fulfillment, we move into a dimension where the smallest quantity is, in a sense, the greatest, and the smallest number, short of nothing, is all-important. The ultimate test of the meaning of what we teach is its implication for the individual person. Meanings may be shared, but they are realized as a personal experience by one person, and by him alone.

The ultimate statistic in the world of the self is not the many, nor even the few, but a statistic in which $N = 1$, and that one is you, or I. This does not mean that the you or the I dwells in isolation in a separate world. The self and the other are closely bound together. But the final repository of meaning is within each person as a separate self.

—And Yet So Great

To those who are accustomed to think of value in terms of quantity, this is a difficult thought. Yet let us pursue it. This self of yours, or this self of mine, what does it count? In number, it is just one among the countless many. In dimension, it is so small in the vast expanse of visible and invisible things. In time, it is bound to a fleeting moment in the eons that have gone before and will follow.

This self—a dot, a speck, a shadow—is from one point of view quite near to nothing.

Yet it is everything.

It is a dot and a shadow, yes, but the shadow of a mighty rock. It is the center of ultimate significance in the life of each person. It is the core of individual existence. It is the only existence you or I can know.

If there is meaning, it is here within myself that I must find it.

If there is value, it is here I must embrace it.

If life is worth living, it is here I must realize its worth.

If there is something in existence that is of ultimate concern, it is here I must cling to it. Here in this self—my self, your self—is where time touches on the eternal. Here the finite and the infinite are joined.

It is through my self—and through your self—that the intimacy of individual existence is realized, and it is also through this self that intimacy and relatedness with others is achieved. The self is the citadel of one's own being and worth and the stronghold from which one moves out to others.

It is to this concept of respect for self and acceptance of self (which is the fountainhead of respect and compassion for others) that this book is devoted. What does this concept

135

mean in practical terms? It means that each teacher will seek as best he can to face himself and to find himself in order to further his own growth. To some this may mean, as an initial step, an effort to grow in self-discovery through group experiences in educational settings, which are becoming more widely available; some may wish to enter group therapy; some may seek individual therapy. These are among the personal expedients. More fundamental is the idea that to encourage the process of self-discovery, we must raise the question of personal significance in connection with everything we seek to learn and everything that is taught from the nursery school through postgraduate years. What does it mean? What difference does it make? What is there in the lessons we teach, the exercises we assign, the books we read, the experiences we enter into, and in all of our undertakings, that can help us to find ourselves and, through us, help others in their search?

Bibliography

Bibliography

1. Adler, A. *The Practice and Theory of Individual Psychology.* Tr. by P. Raden. New York: Harcourt, 1929.
2. Alexander, H. B. *Odes on the Generations of Man.* New York: Baker & Taylor, 1910.
3. Ephron, B. K. *Emotional Difficulties in Reading.* New York: Julian Press, 1953.
4. Fleege, W. H. *Self-Revelations of the Adolescent Boy.* Milwaukee: Bruce Pub., 1944.
5. Freeman, L. *Hope for the Troubled.* New York: Crown, 1953.
6. Freud, S. *The Basic Writings of Sigmund Freud.* Ed. by A. A. Brill. New York: Modern Library, 1938.
7. Freud, S. *New Introductory Lectures on Psycho-Analysis.* Tr. by W. J. H. Sprott. New York: Norton, 1933.
8. Freud, S. *The Problem of Anxiety.* New York: Norton, 1936.
9. Fromm, E. *Escape from Freedom.* New York: Rinehart, 1941.
10. Fromm, E. *Man for Himself.* New York: Rinehart, 1947.
11. Gershman, H. "The Problem of Anxiety." *American Journal of Psychoanalysis,* 10: 89–91, 1950.
12. Havighurst, R. J., and H. Taba. *Adolescent Character and Personality.* New York: John Witty, 1949.
13. Hertzman, J. "High School Mental Hygiene Survey." *American Journal of Orthopsychiatry,* 18: 238–256, April 1948.
14. Hoch, P. H., and J. Zubin, eds. *Anxiety.* New York: Grune and Stratton, 1950.
15. Horney, K. "On Feeling Abused." *American Journal of Psychoanalysis,* 11: 5–12, 1951.
16. Horney, K. *Neurosis and Human Growth.* New York: Norton, 1950.
17. Horney, K. *The Neurotic Personality of Our Time.* New York: Norton, 1937.
18. Horney, K. *New Ways in Psychoanalysis.* New York: Norton, 1939.
19. Horney, K. *Our Inner Conflicts.* New York: Norton, 1945.
20. Jersild, A. T. *Child Psychology.* 4th ed. New York: Prentice-Hall, 1954.

21. Jersild, A. T. "Discipline." *Baltimore Bulletin of Education*, 31: 27–32, April 1954.
22. Jersild, A. T. "Emotional Development." *Manual of Child Psychology*. Ed. by L. Carmichael. Rev. ed. New York: Wiley, 1954. Chap. xiv.
23. Jersild, A. T. *In Search of Self*. New York: Bureau of Publications, Teachers College, Columbia University, 1952.
24. Jersild, A. T. "Self-Understanding in Childhood and Adolescence." *American Psychologist*, 6: 122–126, April 1951.
25. Jersild, A. T. "Understanding Others through Facing Ourselves." *Childhood Education*, 30: 411–414, May 1954.
26. Jersild, A. T., B. Goldman, and J. Loftus. "A Comparative Study of the Worries of Children in Two School Situations." *Journal of Experimental Education*, 9: 323–326, 353, June 1941.
27. Jersild, A. T., K. Helfant, and associates. *Education for Self-Understanding*. New York: Bureau of Publications, Teachers College, Columbia University, 1953.
28. Jersild, A. T., and F. B. Holmes. *Children's Fears*. Child Development Monographs No. 20. New York: Bureau of Publications, Teachers College, Columbia University, 1935.
29. Jung, C. G. *Contributions to Analytical Psychology*. Tr. by H. G. and C. F. Baynes. New York: Harcourt, 1928.
30. Jung, C. G. *Collected Papers on Analytical Psychology*. Ed. by C. E. Long. 2d. ed. London: Baillière, 1922.
31. Jung, C. G. *Modern Man in Search of a Soul*. London: Kegan Paul, Trench, Trubner & Co., 1933.
32. Kierkegaard, S. *Concluding Unscientific Postscript*. Tr. by W. Lowrie. Princeton, N. J.: Princeton University Press, 1941.
33. Kierkegaard, S. *Either/Or*. Tr. by W. Lowrie. Princeton, N. J.: Princeton University Press, 1949.
34. Kierkegaard, S. *Fear and Trembling*. Tr. by W. Lowrie. Princeton, N. J.: Princeton University Press, 1954.
35. Kierkegaard, S. *The Sickness unto Death*. Tr. by W. Lowrie. Princeton, N. J.: Princeton University Press, 1951.
36. Kierkegaard, S. *Works of Love*. Tr. by W. Lowrie. Princeton, N. J.: Princeton University Press, 1949.
37. Lawrence, D. H. *Studies in Classic American Literature*. Garden City, L. I.: Doubleday, 1953.
38. May, R. *The Meaning of Anxiety*. New York: Ronald Press, 1950.
39. Murphy, G. "The Freeing of Intelligence." *Psychological Bulletin*, 42: 1–19, January 1945.
40. Penty, R. C. *Reading Ability and High School Drop-outs*. New York: Bureau of Publications, Teachers College, Columbia University, 1956.

41. Powell, M. G. "Comparison of Self-Ratings, Peer Ratings, and Expert Ratings of Personality Adjustment." *Educational and Psychological Measurements,* 8: 225–234, Summer 1948.
42. Roberts, D. E. *Psychotherapy and a Christian View of Man.* New York: Scribner, 1950.
43. Roe, A. *The Making of a Scientist.* New York: Dodd, 1953.
44. Rogers, C. R. *Counseling and Psychotherapy: Newer Concepts in Practice.* Boston, Houghton, 1942.
45. Rogers, C. R. "A Study of the Mental Health Problems in Three Representative Elementary Schools." *A Study of Health and Physical Education in Columbus Public Schools.* Monographs of the Bureau of Educational Research, No. 25. Columbus: Ohio State University Press, 1942. P. 130–161.
46. Ross, M. G. *Religious Beliefs of Youth.* New York: Association Press, 1950.
47. Spivack, S. S. "A Study of a Method of Appraising Self-Acceptance and Self-Rejection." *Journal of Genetic Psychology.* In press.
48. Sullivan, H. S. *Conceptions of Modern Psychiatry.* Washington, D. C.: William Alanson White Psychiatric Foundation, 1947.
49. Sullivan, H. S. *The Interpersonal Theory of Psychiatry.* New York: Norton, 1953.
50. Sullivan, H. S. *The Meaning of Anxiety in Psychiatry and in Life.* New York: William Alanson White Institute of Psychiatry, 1948.
51. Symonds, P. M., and M. Sherman. "Personality Survey of a Junior High School." *The Measurement of Student Adjustment and Achievement.* Ed. by W. T. Donahue and others. Ann Arbor: University of Michigan Press, 1949. P. 23–50.
52. Tillich, P. *The Courage to Be.* New Haven, Conn.: Yale University Press, 1952.
53. Tillich, P. *Shaking the Foundations.* New York: Scribner, 1953.
54. Ullman, C. A. *Identification of Maladjusted School Children: A Comparison of Three Methods of Screening.* Public Health Monograph, No. 7. Washington, D. C.: Government Printing Office, 1952.
55. Wenkart, A. "Self-Acceptance." *American Journal of Psychoanalysis,* 15: 135–143, October 1955.
56. Wickman, E. K. *Children's Behavior and Teachers' Attitudes.* New York: Commonwealth Fund, 1928.

Appendixes

A. Self-Understanding

Do not sign your name.   *Sex:* Male _____   Female _____

Age: 20–30 _____ 30–40 _____
Over 40 _____

Marital Status: Single _____
Married (inc. widowed or divorced) _____

1. The idea that a major goal in education should be to help young people to understand themselves and to develop healthy attitudes of self-acceptance
   a. _____ Makes me feel uneasy and resistant.
   b. _____ Is challenging, but I doubt its practicability.
   c. _____ Is promising and worth trying.

2. The idea that to help young people to understand themselves it is necessary also for the teacher to be involved in the process of growing in self-understanding strikes me as being
   a. _____ Rather unpleasant and distasteful.
   b. _____ Quite sensible, but probably not much could come of it.
   c. _____ Challenging and promising from the point of view of my own personal and professional growth.

3. Assuming that the theory has merit and is relevant to your role (as a teacher, nurse, clergyman, etc.), what are the main obstacles? (Check as many or as few items as you wish.)
   a. _____ I am not prepared to venture into this area.
   b. _____ My load as a teacher is already heavy enough.
   c. _____ The administrative set-up makes it impractical.
   d. _____ There may be obstacles, but none great enough to keep me from at least trying.

4. If you feel favorably disposed to the idea, what provisions would you wish for? (Mark one item or several.)

    a. _____ Workshops, special courses, seminars, etc.

    b. _____ Better arrangements for discussing personal and emotional aspects of the teacher's work.

    c. _____ Specialized psychological services for the students.

    d. _____ Help of a distinctly personal sort, such as might be gotten from group therapy.

    e. _____ Other?

Any other comments?

Responses to Questionnaire on Self-Understanding

	A N=78	B N=77	C N=68	D N=73	E N=139	F N=149	G N=33	H N=96	I N=90	J N=145	K N=84
Group*:	%	%	%	%	%	%	%	%	%	%	%
1. The idea that schools should promote self-understanding											
a. Makes me uneasy, resistant	1	0	0	3	0	0	0	0	0	0	1
b. Is challenging but impracticable	3	13	6	0	5	7	0	0	0	4	2
c. Is promising and worth trying	96	87	94	96†	94	92	100	96	94	95	95
2. The idea that understanding others is tied to self-understanding is											
a. Unpleasant and distasteful	0	0	0	1	0	0	0	0	0	.7	0
b. Sensible but not promising	8	12	4	10	7	3	3	0	0	3	2
c. Challenging and promising to me	92	84	96	88	91	97	94	94	93	94	96
3. Obstacles:											
a. I am not prepared	10	8	7	12	17	12	15	21	30	13	21
b. My load is already too heavy	10	27	12	15	8	10	0	13	11	10	4
c. Administrative set-up prevents	13	27	26	19	24	28	6	17	7	21	15
d. No obstacle can fully prevent	73	65	74	71	79	63	85	86	56	81	80
4. Help or provisions personally desired:											
a. Workshops, special courses, etc.	49	23	72	41	43	47	42	51	56	53	37
b. Discussion of personal and emotional issues	63	49	50	40	63	40	64	35	51	67	60
c. Psychological services for others	50	62	54	48	45	48	27	51	33	54	49
d. Personal help, such as group therapy	54	45	28	16	51	24	48	46	32	54	56
b or *d* or both	81	66	54	49	83	54	82	72	60	86	79

* Key to groups appears on page 148.
† When percentages total less than 100, some people did not respond to the item. When percentages total more than 100, some checked more than one alternative.

Key to Groups *

A: Students in a course on the psychology of late adolescence, taught by the writer, which emphasized the need for knowing oneself if one would understand others.

B: High school teachers who responded to the questionnaire after a twenty-minute talk and a twenty-five-minute group discussion of the implications of understanding of self for understanding others.

C: Students in a course on the psychology of early adolescence, in which the concept of selfhood was not stressed and some critical reservations were made concerning the concept of self-understanding.

D: Students in a course on the psychology of late adolescence, as in C.

E: Students in a Foundations of Education course in which emphasis was given about equally to (a) theory of learning, (b) sociological factors in personal development, and (c) the concept of selfhood and the implications of self-understanding.

F: Students in a Foundations of Education course (as in E) with considerable emphasis on understanding forces in one's own development. Limited experience with group therapy (under the leadership of advanced students in clinical psychology) was provided for those who desired it.

G: Students in a seminar on problems of curriculum and teaching, who responded to the questionnaire after a thirty-minute talk and a twenty-minute discussion (plus preliminary reading) concerning the implications of self-understanding.

H: Students in a Foundations of Education course, as in E.

I: Students in an educational psychology course in which no introduction to the concepts of selfhood and self-understanding had been given.

J: Students in a course on the psychology of adolescence, taught by the writer, as in A.

K: Students in a course on the psychology of the elementary school child, taught by the writer, as in A.

* Student groups consisted mainly of graduate students.

B. Personal Issues
Inventory

During the past year about a thousand people have responded to the preceding questionnaire.* Many of those who checked item 4*b* (pertaining to personal and emotional concerns) or 4*d* (the idea that group therapy might be valuable) have mentioned some of the issues in their lives they would like to understand more fully. The items below have been taken from statements by these people.

Please look at each statement, noting whether it expresses a feeling or an issue you have experienced in your own life, and check whether you would like to have a deeper understanding of its personal meaning, or whether it does not seem to be an important issue.

In the statements there are some themes that recur, but this does not mean that there is any correct or consistent pattern of answers. Consider each statement by itself and note whether, in the way it is phrased, it happens to express a problem or feeling of your own.

What others have said: "This is an issue in my personal life and I would like, if possible, to gain a deeper understanding of what it means."

"It is difficult for me to see myself as one who might seek and accept help in dealing with life's problems. I guess I feel that I should have the strength and ability to handle personal problems without help."

My own feeling, as I consider what I'd like to understand about myself, is that:

I've felt this way, and it's one of the areas in which I probably need help in understanding myself. _____

I've felt this way, but I don't particularly see it as an issue on which I need help. _____

This has not been an issue in my life. _____

I'm not sure. _____

* This Inventory, which was used with Groups J and K, was preceded by the questionnaire shown in Appendix A.

149

What others have said:

"I feel a great need to compare myself with others and to assure myself that I am superior to others or at least as good."

My own feeling:

I've felt this way, and it's one of the areas in which I probably need help in understanding myself. _____

I've felt this way, but I don't particularly see it as an issue on which I need help. _____

This has not been an issue in my life. _____

I'm not sure. _____

What others have said:

"I feel that the opportunity for the right kind of sex experience has not come my way."

My own feeling:

I've felt this way, and it's one of the areas in which I probably need help in understanding myself. _____

I've felt this way, but I don't particularly see it as an issue on which I need help. _____

This has not been an issue in my life. _____

I'm not sure. _____

What others have said:

"I'm not really sure of what I want from life—I don't seem to be convinced of what is most important to do, or to be, or to get from life."

My own feeling:

I've felt this way, and it's one of the areas in which I probably need help in understanding myself. _____

I've felt this way, but I don't particularly see it as an issue on which I need help. _____

This has not been an issue in my life. _____

I'm not sure. _____

What others have said:

"It is hard for me to feel as free to be myself in my relations with people who are higher than I in position or rank or prestige as with people who are equal to me or of lower position."

My own feeling:

I've felt this way, and it's one of the areas in which I probably need help in understanding myself. _____

I've felt this way, but I don't particularly see it as an issue on which I need help. _____

This has not been an issue in my life. _____

I'm not sure. _____

150

What others have said:

"Although I believe life's struggle may be worth while, it often seems rather hopeless."

My own feeling:

I've felt this way, and it's one of the areas in which I probably need help in understanding myself. ———

I've felt this way, but I don't particularly see it as an issue on which I need help. ———

This has not been an issue in my life. ———

I'm not sure. ———

What others have said:

"I spend a good deal of my professional life in an atmosphere that is impersonal, and all the people seem to be rather remote from one another."

My own feeling:

I've felt this way, and it's one of the areas in which I probably need help in understanding myself. ———

I've felt this way, but I don't particularly see it as an issue on which I need help. ———

This has not been an issue in my life. ———

I'm not sure. ———

What others have said:

"Even though I try to get along smoothly with others, so often other people don't really consider my feelings."

My own feeling:

I've felt this way, and it's one of the areas in which I probably need help in understanding myself. ———

I've felt this way, but I don't particularly see it as an issue on which I need help. ———

This has not been an issue in my life. ———

I'm not sure. ———

What others have said:

"I feel that I have been quite lucky in life, on the whole; such success as I have had has been due to a large degree to good fortune and the good will of others, and I sometimes wonder whether my luck will run out."

My own feeling:

I've felt this way, and it's one of the areas in which I probably need help in understanding myself. ———

I've felt this way, but I don't particularly see it as an issue on which I need help. ———

This has not been an issue in my life. ———

I'm not sure. ———

151

What others have said:

"I feel that there are important things in life I have missed and never will find, no matter how hard I try or how much I accomplish."

My own feeling:

I've felt this way, and it's one of the areas in which I probably need help in understanding myself. _____

I've felt this way, but I don't particularly see it as an issue on which I need help. _____

This has not been an issue in my life. _____

I'm not sure. _____

What others have said:

"I tend to get involved in so many activities and responsibilities that I don't have much time for myself."

My own feeling:

I've felt this way, and it's one of the areas in which I probably need help in understanding myself. _____

I've felt this way, but I don't particularly see it as an issue on which I need help. _____

This has not been an issue in my life. _____

I'm not sure. _____

What others have said:

"Somehow I don't seem to be able to free myself from feelings of blame or guilt concerning the kinds of sex experience I have had."

My own feeling:

I've felt this way, and it's one of the areas in which I probably need help in understanding myself. _____

I've felt this way, but I don't particularly see it as an issue on which I need help. _____

This has not been an issue in my life. _____

I'm not sure. _____

What others have said:

"I seem to go from one job or relationship or place to another without finding what I seem to be seeking."

My own feeling:

I've felt this way, and it's one of the areas in which I probably need help in understanding myself. _____

I've felt this way, but I don't particularly see it as an issue on which I need help. _____

This has not been an issue in my life. _____

I'm not sure. _____

What others have said:

"I often feel I am required to give the impression of being more able, or more strong, or more considerate, or more independent than I have capacity for. I keep feeling I cannot live up to what others expect of me."

What others have said:

"Loneliness is one of the feelings that I often have."

What others have said:

"I feel that while maybe I once had a home (in a physical and psychological sense), I have lost this home and haven't found another."

What others have said:

"Somehow I do not seem to be able to free myself from a feeling of inadequacy (or shame or guilt) because of the kinds of sex experiences I have *not* had in the past."

My own feeling:

I've felt this way, and it's one of the areas in which I probably need help in understanding myself. _____

I've felt this way, but I don't particularly see it as an issue on which I need help. _____

This has not been an issue in my life. _____

I'm not sure. _____

My own feeling:

I've felt this way, and it's one of the areas in which I probably need help in understanding myself. _____

I've felt this way, but I don't particularly see it as an issue on which I need help. _____

This has not been an issue in my life. _____

I'm not sure. _____

My own feeling:

I've felt this way, and it's one of the areas in which I probably need help in understanding myself. _____

I've felt this way, but I don't particularly see it as an issue on which I need help. _____

This has not been an issue in my life. _____

I'm not sure. _____

My own feeling:

I've felt this way, and it's one of the areas in which I probably need help in understanding myself. _____

I've felt this way, but I don't particularly see it as an issue on which I need help. _____

This has not been an issue in my life. _____

I'm not sure. _____

What others have said:

"I know in theory that it is good to be able to have the freedom to feel one's anger, love, fear, joy, grief, etc., but I don't think I see what implications this has for me."

My own feeling:

I've felt this way, and it's one of the areas in which I probably need help in understanding myself. _____

I've felt this way, but I don't particularly see it as an issue on which I need help. _____

This has not been an issue in my life. _____

I'm not sure. _____

What others have said:

"When I'm with my own people at home I feel there is something lacking there and when I associate with people outside my home I also feel there is something lacking in them—I don't seem to feel settled or to have roots anywhere."

My own feeling:

I've felt this way, and it's one of the areas in which I probably need help in understanding myself. _____

I've felt this way, but I don't particularly see it as an issue on which I need help. _____

This has not been an issue in my life. _____

I'm not sure. _____

What others have said:

"I feel cut off from others too much; I might say there is an invisible barrier between me and others."

My own feeling:

I've felt this way, and it's one of the areas in which I probably need help in understanding myself. _____

I've felt this way, but I don't particularly see it as an issue on which I need help. _____

This has not been an issue in my life. _____

I'm not sure. _____

What others have said:

"Quite often when someone asks me to do something or go somewhere or take some sort of responsibility I say Yes and then afterwards I regret it or feel annoyed about having said Yes."

My own feeling:

I've felt this way, and it's one of the areas in which I probably need help in understanding myself. _____

I've felt this way, but I don't particularly see it as an issue on which I need help. _____

This has not been an issue in my life. _____

I'm not sure. _____

What others have said:

"I feel that I have never lived up to my ambitions and ideals and often I think I never will."

My own feeling:

I've felt this way, and it's one of the areas in which I probably need help in understanding myself. _____

I've felt this way, but I don't particularly see it as an issue on which I need help. _____

This has not been an issue in my life. _____

I'm not sure. _____

What others have said:

"In my work (teaching, nursing, homemaking, etc.) I often have to get others to do or learn things that to me don't seem very meaningful or important."

My own feeling:

I've felt this way, and it's one of the areas in which I probably need help in understanding myself. _____

I've felt this way, but I don't particularly see it as an issue on which I need help. _____

This has not been an issue in my life. _____

I'm not sure. _____

What others have said:

"I feel that my family demands or has demanded things of me to an extent that I resent, yet I don't seem to be able to assert my own wishes or feel that I have a perfect right to rebel."

My own feeling:

I've felt this way, and it's one of the areas in which I probably need help in understanding myself. _____

I've felt this way, but I don't particularly see it as an issue on which I need help. _____

This has not been an issue in my life. _____

I'm not sure. _____

What others have said:

"I have a feeling that one must be on guard and not take things lying down, for people will take advantage of you."

My own feeling:

I've felt this way, and it's one of the areas in which I probably need help in understanding myself. _____

I've felt this way, but I don't particularly see it as an issue on which I need help. _____

This has not been an issue in my life. _____

I'm not sure. _____

155

What others have said:

"I sometimes feel that life is so complicated and mixed up that I wonder whether it is worth while to keep up the struggle."

My own feeling:

I've felt this way, and it's one of the areas in which I probably need help in understanding myself. _____

I've felt this way, but I don't particularly see it as an issue on which I need help. _____

This has not been an issue in my life. _____

I'm not sure. _____

What others have said:

"I sometimes feel that it might be too disillusioning and perhaps even frightening for me really to come to understand myself."

My own feeling:

I've felt this way, and it's one of the areas in which I probably need help in understanding myself. _____

I've felt this way, but I don't particularly see it as an issue on which I need help. _____

This has not been an issue in my life. _____

I'm not sure. _____

What others have said:

"It makes me feel uneasy when others show their feelings (such as rage, tenderness, or fear) in public or come to me and openly lay bare their feelings."

My own feeling:

I've felt this way, and it's one of the areas in which I probably need help in understanding myself. _____

I've felt this way, but I don't particularly see it as an issue on which I need help. _____

This has not been an issue in my life. _____

I'm not sure. _____

What others have said:

"I sometimes feel as though I tend to judge my personality as a whole on the basis of what has happened or is lacking in my sex life."

My own feeling:

I've felt this way, and it's one of the areas in which I probably need help in understanding myself. _____

I've felt this way, but I don't particularly see it as an issue on which I need help. _____

This has not been an issue in my life. _____

I'm not sure. _____

156

What others have said:

"I sometimes lose my temper or have feelings of anger or intense rage that disturb me."

My own feeling:

I've felt this way, and it's one of the areas in which I probably need help in understanding my-self. _____

I've felt this way, but I don't particularly see it as an issue on which I need help. _____

This has not been an issue in my life. _____

I'm not sure. _____

What others have said:

"I feel that there are things in life I have had to give up, and I suspect that at my age it is too late to make up for them."

My own feeling:

I've felt this way, and it's one of the areas in which I probably need help in understanding my-self. _____

I've felt this way, but I don't particularly see it as an issue on which I need help. _____

This has not been an issue in my life. _____

I'm not sure. _____

What others have said:

"I often feel bitter and re-sentful at being pushed around or imposed on by others with-out being free to complain or show my resentment."

My own feeling:

I've felt this way, and it's one of the areas in which I probably need help in understanding my-self. _____

I've felt this way, but I don't particularly see it as an issue on which I need help. _____

This has not been an issue in my life. _____

I'm not sure. _____

What others have said:

"What I'm doing and what is happening in my life doesn't seem to mean much to me. I would like to feel good about my endeavors (such as my job, or my studies, or my family or community activities), but I can't say I really do."

My own feeling:

I've felt this way, and it's one of the areas in which I probably need help in understanding my-self. _____

I've felt this way, but I don't particularly see it as an issue on which I need help. _____

This has not been an issue in my life. _____

I'm not sure. _____

What others have said:

"I have no one to whom I can confide my innermost feelings about things that concern me deeply, knowing that I will be listened to or understood."

My own feeling:

I've felt this way, and it's one of the areas in which I probably need help in understanding myself. _____

I've felt this way, but I don't particularly see it as an issue on which I need help. _____

This has not been an issue in my life. _____

I'm not sure. _____

What others have said:

"In making decisions or in thinking about a step I have taken, I often ask myself what someone else (a parent or friend or department head or senior colleague) would have done in a similar situation."

My own feeling:

I've felt this way, and it's one of the areas in which I probably need help in understanding myself. _____

I've felt this way, but I don't particularly see it as an issue on which I need help. _____

This has not been an issue in my life. _____

I'm not sure. _____

What others have said:

"Whether I'm at work or at home or on vacation, I somehow feel at loose ends and don't feel as if I really belong."

My own feeling:

I've felt this way, and it's one of the areas in which I probably need help in understanding myself. _____

I've felt this way, but I don't particularly see it as an issue on which I need help. _____

This has not been an issue in my life. _____

I'm not sure. _____

From my point of view, issues of the sort raised above

_____ May be disturbing, but it is better to raise them than to ignore them.

_____ Are disturbing or lead to all sorts of introspection, and it is better not to bother with them.

_____ Don't matter much, as I see it.

C. Categories

The nine categories included in the Personal Issues Inventory and the four statements used for each category appear below. The number of people selecting Option 1 ("I've felt this way, and it's one of the areas in which I probably need help in understanding myself") is shown in parentheses following each statement.

LONELINESS

Loneliness is one of the feelings that I often have. (63)

I feel cut off from others too much; I might say there is an invisible barrier between me and others. (48)

I have no one to whom I can confide my innermost feelings about things that concern me deeply, knowing that I will be listened to or understood. (37)

I spend a good deal of my professional life in an atmosphere that is impersonal, and all the people seem to be rather remote from one another. (26)

MEANINGLESSNESS

I'm not really sure of what I want from life—I don't seem to be convinced of what is most important to do, or to be, or to get from life. (82)

I tend to get involved in so many activities and responsibilities that I don't have much time for myself. (40)

What I'm doing and what is happening in my life doesn't seem to mean much to me. I would like to feel good about my endeavors (such as my job, or my studies, or my family or community activities), but I can't say I really do. (35)

In my work (teaching, nursing, homemaking, etc.) I often have to get others to do or learn things that to me don't seem very meaningful or important. (27)

ATTITUDES TOWARD AUTHORITY

It is hard for me to feel as free to be myself in my relations with people who are higher than I in position or rank or prestige as with people who are equal to me or of lower position. (76)

Quite often when someone asks me to do something or go somewhere or take some sort of responsibility I say Yes and then afterwards I regret it or feel annoyed about having said Yes. (57)

I feel that my family demands or has demanded things of me to an extent that I resent, yet I don't seem to be able to assert my own wishes or feel that I have a perfect right to rebel. (41)

In making decisions or in thinking about a step I have taken I often ask myself what someone else (a parent or friend or department head or senior colleague) would have done in a similar situation. (40)

Conflict Relating to Sex

I feel that the opportunity for the right kind of sex experience has not come my way. (37)

Somehow I don't seem to be able to free myself from feelings of blame or guilt concerning the kinds of sex experience I have had. (33)

I sometimes feel as though I tend to judge my personality as a whole on the basis of what has happened or is lacking in my sex life. (32)

Somehow I do not seem to be able to free myself from a feeling of inadequacy (or shame or guilt) because of the kinds of sex experiences I have *not* had in the past. (21)

Hostility

I sometimes lose my temper or have feelings of anger or intense rage that disturb me. (65)

I often feel bitter and resentful at being pushed around or imposed on by others without being free to complain or show my resentment. (40)

Even though I try to get along smoothly with others, so often other people don't really consider my feelings. (34)

I have a feeling that one must be on guard and not take things lying down, for people will take advantage of you. (19)

Discrepancy between Real and Ideal

I often feel I am required to give the impression of being more able, or more strong, or more considerate, or more independent than I have capacity for. I keep feeling I cannot live up to what others expect of me. (82)

I feel a great need to compare myself with others and to assure myself that I am superior to others or at least as good. (72)

I feel that I have never lived up to my ambitions and ideals and often I think I never will. (51)

I something feel that it might be too disillusioning and perhaps even frightening for me really to come to understand myself. (39)

Lack of Freedom to Feel

It is difficult for me to see myself as one who might seek and accept help in dealing with life's problems.   feel that I should have the strength and ability to handle personal problems without help. (74)

I know in theory that it is good to be able to have the freedom to feel one's anger, love, fear, joy, grief, etc., but I don't think I see what implications this has for me. (44)

It makes me feel uneasy when others show their feelings (such as rage, tenderness, or fear) in public or come to me and openly lay bare their feelings. (38)

I feel that I have been quite lucky in life, on the whole; such success as I have had has been due to a large degree to good fortune and the good will of others, and I sometimes wonder whether my luck will run out. (19)

Hopelessness

I feel that there are important things in life I have missed and never will find, no matter how hard I try or how much I accomplish. (39)

I feel that there are things in life I have had to give up, and I suspect that at my age it is too late to make up for them. (39)

Although I believe life's struggle may be worth while, it often seems . rather hopeless. (37)

I sometimes feel that life is so complicated and mixed up that I wonder whether it is worth while to keep up the struggle. (28)

Homelessness

I seem to go from one job or relationship or place to another without finding what I seem to be seeking. (40)

Whether I'm at work or at home or on vacation, I somehow feel at loose ends and don't feel as if I really belong. (36)

When I'm with my own people at home I feel there is something lacking there and when I associate with people outside my home I also feel there is something lacking in them—I don't seem to feel settled or to have roots anywhere. (29)

I feel that while maybe I once had a home (in a physical and psychological sense) I have lost this home and haven't found another. (24)

D. Responses to Personal Issues Inventory

TABLE 1

PERCENTAGE, BY CATEGORY, OF PEOPLE IN GROUP J (N = 145)
CHECKING AT LEAST ONE STATEMENT IN THAT CATEGORY AS REPRESENTING A PROBLEM ON WHICH THEY PROBABLY NEEDED HELP

Category	People who had previously indicated a desire for help by checking 4d alone or in conjunction with 4b* on questionnaire shown in Appendix A			People who had checked neither 4d nor 4b			People who had checked 4b only		
	Men N=36	Women N=42	Total N=78	Men N=9	Women N=10	Total N=19	Men N=19	Women N=29	Total N=48
	%	%	%	%	%	%	%	%	%
Loneliness	45	55	50	33	50	42	42	37	40
Meaninglessness	56	72	64	66	50	58	53	37	44
Attitudes toward Authority	50	71	59	44	70	58	58	41	48
Conflict Relating to Sex	42	43	42	33	20	26	27	17	21
Hostility	36	48	42	66	60	63	58	48	52
Discrepancy between Real and Ideal	62	70	65	66	60	63	69	48	56
Lack of Freedom to Feel	62	65	63	44	60	53	32	44	40
Hopelessness	22	43	35	44	40	42	48	20	31
Homelessness	34	38	36	55	40	47	42	34	38

* 4b: Desire arrangements for discussing personal and emotional aspects of their work; 4d: desire help such as group therapy.

TABLE 2

Percentage, by Category, of People in Group K (N = 84) Checking at Least One Statement in That Category as Representing a Problem on Which They Probably Needed Help

Category	People who had previously indicated a desire for help by checking 4d alone or in conjunction with 4b* on questionnaire shown in Appendix A			People who had checked neither 4b nor 4d			People who had checked 4b only		
	Men N = 12 %	Women N = 36 %	Total N = 48 %	Men N = 1 %	Women N = 13 %	Total N = 14 %	Men N = 3 %	Women N = 19 %	Total N = 22 %
Loneliness	58	56	56	0	39	36	66	27	32
Meaninglessness	66	62	63	0	62	57	66	69	68
Attitudes toward Authority	66	70	67	0	39	36	33	42	41
Conflict Relating to Sex	58	39	44	0	15	14	33	32	32
Hostility	66	42	48	0	23	21	66	37	41
Discrepancy between Real and Ideal	66	76	73	0	62	57	33	48	45
Lack of Freedom to Feel	83	64	67	0	39	36	99	74	77
Hopelessness	75	39	48	0	23	21	66	32	36
Homelessness	33	36	35	0	23	21	66	32	36

* 4b: Desire arrangements for discussing personal and emotional aspects of their work; 4d: desire help such as group therapy.

163

TABLE 3

PERCENTAGE, BY CATEGORY, OF PEOPLE IN GROUPS J AND K
(N = 229, INCLUDING 80 MEN AND 149 WOMEN) WHO RESPONDED
TO AT LEAST ONE STATEMENT IN THAT CATEGORY
BY CHECKING OPTION 1 OR OPTION 2

Category	Option 1: I've felt this way, and it's one of the areas in which I probably need help in understanding myself	Option 2: I've felt this way, but I don't particularly see it as an issue on which I need help	Option 1 or Option 2
	%	%	%
Loneliness	46	29	75
Meaninglessness	59	33	92
Attitudes toward Authority	55	34	89
Conflict Relating to Sex	34	22	56
Hostility	46	33	79
Discrepancy between Real and Ideal	62	23	85
Lack of Freedom to Feel	59	25	84
Hopelessness	37	35	72
Homelessness	36	21	57

TABLE 4

Number of People in Groups J and K (N = 229) Checking Option 1
or Option 2 in Responding to the Thirty-six Statements
on the Personal Issues Inventory*

Statement	Option 1: I've felt this way, and it's one of the areas in which I probably need help in understanding myself	Option 2: I've felt this way, but I don't particularly see it as an issue on which I need help
I'm not really sure of what I want from life—I don't seem to be convinced of what is most important to do, or to be, or to get from life.	82	57
I often feel I am required to give the impression of being more able, or more strong, or more considerate, or more independent than I have capacity for. I keep feeling I cannot live up to what others expect of me.	82	38
It is hard for me to feel as free to be myself in my relations with people who are higher than I in position or rank or prestige as with people who are equal to me or of lower position.	76	52
It is difficult for me to see myself as one who might seek and accept help in dealing with life's problems. I guess I feel that I should have the strength and ability to handle personal problems without help.	74	41
I feel a great need to compare myself with others and to assure myself that I am superior to others or at least as good.	72	42
I sometimes lose my temper or have feelings of anger or intense rage that disturb me.	65	51
Loneliness is one of the feelings that I often have.	63	67
Quite often when someone asks me to do something or go somewhere or take some sort of responsibility I say Yes and then afterwards I regret it or feel annoyed about having said Yes.	57	69

* Statements are listed in order of frequency under Option 1.

TABLE 4 (*Continued*)

Statement	Option 1: I've felt this way, and it's one of the areas in which I probably need help in understanding myself	Option 2: I've felt this way, but I don't particularly see it as an issue on which I need help
I feel that I have never lived up to my ambitions and ideals and often I think I never will.	51	47
I feel cut off from others too much; I might say there is an invisible barrier between me and others.	48	26
I know in theory that it is good to be able to have the freedom to feel one's anger, love, fear, joy, grief, etc., but I don't think I see what implications this has for me.	44	32
I feel that my family demands or has demanded things of me to an extent that I resent, yet I don't seem to be able to assert my own wishes or feel that I have a perfect right to rebel.	41	38
I seem to go from one job or relationship or place to another without finding what I seem to be seeking.	40	23
I tend to get involved in so many activities and responsibilities that I don't have much time for myself.	40	66
I often feel bitter and resentful at being pushed around or imposed on by others without being free to complain or show my resentment.	40	45
In making decisions or in thinking about a step I have taken, I often ask myself what someone else (a parent or friend or department head or senior colleague) would have done in a similar situation.	40	71
I sometimes feel that it might be too disillusioning and perhaps even frightening for me really to come to understand myself.	39	17
I feel that there are important things in life I have missed and never will find, no matter how hard I try or how much I accomplish.	39	54

TABLE 4 (*Continued*)

Statement	Option 1: I've felt this way, and it's one of the areas in which I probably need help in understanding myself	Option 2: I've felt this way, but I don't particularly see it as an issue on which I need help
I feel that there are things in life I have had to give up, and I suspect that at my age it is too late to make up for them.	39	44
It makes me feel uneasy when others show their feelings (such as rage, tenderness, or fear) in public or come to me and openly lay bare their feelings.	38	56
Although I believe life's struggle may be worth while, it often seems rather hopeless.	37	51
I feel that the opportunity for the right kind of sex experience has not come my way.	37	37
I have no one to whom I can confide my innermost feelings about things that concern me deeply, knowing that I will be listened to or understood.	37	33
Whether I'm at work or at home or on vacation, I somehow feel at loose ends and don't feel as if I really belong.	36	32
What I'm doing and what is happening in my life doesn't seem to mean much to me. I would like to feel good about my endeavors (such as my job, or my studies, or my family or community activities), but I can't say I really do.	35	37
Even though I try to get along smoothly with others, so often other people don't really consider my feelings.	34	47
Somehow I don't seem to be able to free myself from feelings of blame or guilt concerning the kinds of sex experience I have had.	33	27
I sometimes feel as though I tend to judge my personality as a whole on the basis of what has happened or is lacking in my sex life.	32	16

TABLE 4 (*Continued*)

Statement	Option 1: I've felt this way, and it's one of the areas in which I probably need help in understanding myself	Option 2: I've felt this way, but I don't particularly see it as an issue on which I need help
When I'm with my own people at home I feel there is something lacking there and when I associate with people outside my home I also feel there is something lacking in them—I don't seem to feel settled or to have roots anywhere.	29	37
I sometimes feel that life is so complicated and mixed up that I wonder whether it is worth while to keep up the struggle.	28	35
In my work (teaching, nursing, homemaking, etc.) I often have to get others to do or learn things that to me don't seem very meaningful or important.	27	53
I spend a good deal of my professional life in an atmosphere that is impersonal, and all the people seem to be rather remote from one another.	26	28
I feel that while maybe I once had a home (in a physical and psychological sense), I have lost this home and haven't found another.	24	19
Somehow I do not seem to be able to free myself from a feeling of inadequacy (or shame or guilt) because of the kinds of sex experiences I have *not* had in the past.	21	26
I feel that I have been quite lucky in life, on the whole; such success as I have had has been due to a large degree to good fortune and the good will of others, and I sometimes wonder whether my luck will run out.	19	48
I have a feeling that one must be on guard and not take things lying down, for people will take advantage of you.	19	55

E. Reactions to Anxiety

Reactions (in the form of written ratings and evaluations) to lectures and discussions dealing with the personal and educational implications of anxiety were obtained from members of five classes taught by the writer and enrolling from twenty to one hundred and eighty students.

The most systematic effort to obtain reactions was made in Group J (see Appendix A and page 148). A short evaluation blank, which was regularly distributed at the end of class meetings, was distributed also at the end of a session devoted to anxiety. Members could use the blank or ignore it, and respond anonymously or by name. Eighty-nine of the one hundred and forty-five persons who were present at the meeting volunteered an evaluation. This was a larger number than had volunteered evaluations at any other class session. A rating scale, ranging from 10 ("unsurpassed") through 9 ("excellent") and down to the poorest possible rating of 1 was included on the evaluation blank. The median rating of the discussion of anxiety was 9. The lowest rating was 4 ("fair"). Most of these ratings were accompanied by written comments. No session of the course received a higher rating or a larger number of approving comments.

At the following meeting of the class there was an additional call for an informal expression of opinion. It was pointed out that some persons think the issue of anxiety should not be raised with teachers since it might make them anxious without doing them any good. The contrary view was also briefly set forth. Students in the class were then asked to volunteer comments, anonymously and in writing, on this issue. Sixty-three people volunteered written comments, ranging from a sentence or two to lengthy statements. Of these, sixty strongly expressed the view that anxiety was an important and essential concept in education and should be discussed as fully and as openly as possible. Two people were noncommittal and one was negative, saying, "It has little value."

As indicated in Chapter Two, there were many personal reactions to the topic of anxiety that could not readily be treated in a quantitative way.